AF479112

Hey Dad...
is Grandma
a Criminal?

SUSAN HITCHLER
(GRANDMA)

Printed in the United States of America

Edited by Kristen Corrects, Inc.

Cover art design by StandoutBooks.com

First edition published 2019

All quotes from the Bible are taken from the NIV (New International Version) unless otherwise noted.

Paperback: 978-0-578-61056-6
Ebook: 978-0-578-61060-3
Hardcover: 978-0-578-61063-4

"In the shelter of your presence you hide them from all human intrigues; you keep them safe in your dwelling from accusing tongues."

Psalm 31:10

"Resistance to tyranny becomes the Christian and social duty of each individual…

Continue…with your dependence on God…

Nobly defend those rights which Heaven gave and no man ought to take from us."

John Hancock

"If you do not take an interest in the affairs of your government, then you are doomed to live under the rule of fools."

Plato

Contents

Foreword

I have never written a book. Starting to write one at age seventy was not in my retirement plans.

I was a professional speaker and consultant (professional name Susan Stephani). I had always wanted to write a book but never found a compelling reason to write one. Until now.

Being charged with a crime twice by a Waukesha County, Wisconsin prosecutor (when, according to the written law, a crime was never committed) was traumatic. That experience led me to research prosecutor misconduct.

I was shocked at what I discovered. The disturbing information that I found became an exceptionally compelling reason to write a book. I needed to warn people that no one is safe from an abusive prosecutor with a personal, professional, or political agenda. The Center for Prosecutor Integrity calls prosecutor misconduct an epidemic.[1] This epidemic of misconduct has harmed thousands of innocent people across this country.

Writing this book has been an incredible challenge. There is so much to say on every aspect of the harm and havoc that self-serving prosecutors can cause in the life of an innocent person.

What happened to me is a miniscule example of the life-altering experience of being wrongfully charged with a crime. Being convicted, despite being innocent of any crime is devastating.

In *Hey Dad…Is Grandma a Criminal?* I want to inform people who have little or no knowledge of the criminal justice system that totally innocent people can be charged with a crime. I have a goal, a strong desire for others to benefit from my years of research

---

1 Center for Prosecutor Integrity, "An Epidemic of Prosecutor Misconduct," 2013, http://www.prosecutorintegrity.org/wp-content/uploads/EpidemicofProsecutorMisconduct.pdf

untangling the legal and procedural jargon of the United States criminal justice system. It is imperative for every citizen to know what is happening to our justice system, how it is going from a system designed for the safety of the citizens to a system that abuses and uses the citizens.

My hope is that understanding the abuses of the law, rule of law, the Bill of Rights, ethical violations, and the absolute power of prosecutors to charge anyone, anytime, for any reason will motivate more citizens to join in and help to stop this epidemic. You, or someone you love, could be the next innocent person to be wrongfully charged with a crime.

Let's get started.

Susan Hitchler

Introduction

Once Upon A Time...

I believed that our justice system was fair and just. I believed that, in most cases, evidence proved guilt or innocence. I believed that the Constitution of the United States of America and the Bill of Rights were respected and followed. I believed that the constitutional rights of the citizens were unquestionably given and rarely violated. I believed that the law was impartial and fair in most incidences. I believed that we had the best justice system because my country respected the rule of law, the rights of each citizen, and the protection of the innocent.

I believed that until...

I was criminally charged twice—even though the Wisconsin State statutes, i.e. the written law, clearly stated that a crime had not been committed.

Now, I know that anyone can be charged with a crime when there is no evidence of a crime. And, now I know that there is a group of government employees who have legal immunity from most anything they do to innocent citizens for their own personal, professional, or political reasons and not for any legal reason.

From my personal experience and my research on this topic, I have come to learn that prosecutors are presented on TV and in movies as heroes, but in reality, a growing number of them:

- commit violations of the Constitution of the United States and of their individual states
- violate the rule of law
- ignore the law as written by the legislators

- violate due process
- do or would hide evidence from the defense attorney that would clear the innocent person of the crime
- violate ethics rules written especially for prosecutors
- charge someone with a crime when, statutorily, there was never a crime committed
- in general, violate and ignore every safeguard for the citizens intentionally included in the Constitution and the Bill of Rights and, rarely to never, face consequences for doing so.

What I had once believed about our Department of Justice was a fairytale. In reality, no one is safe from experiencing a grave injustice by our justice system.

"We know that the law is good if one uses it properly."

1 Timothy 8

Why Should Anyone Care About an Obscure Case of an Average Citizen?

As you read, I believe you will realize that any citizen of the United States can be used to fulfill a personal, professional, and/or political purpose of a prosecutor. I'm not talking about the high-profile cases with which you may be familiar, like the Duke Lacrosse case or the Walker John Doe case (Wisconsin). I mean anyone!

As you read, I believe that you will begin to understand that what happened to me by tax-paid government employees is happening, and *has* happened, all over this country and at every level of the DOJ to people who are innocent of any crime.

Organization of This Book

First – What? I tell my story. During the yearlong event and even more in the years following, I came to develop insights regarding my case. There are also legal matters that I later understood much more clearly.

Then – So What? I share what I discovered in my five years of research into prosecutor misconduct, including some of the insights I gained and conclusions I reached regarding our justice system. Included as well is how the Judicial Branch of our government was originally designed to function. I am far from the only person who has reached these conclusions.

Finally – Now What? I discuss some of the steps that can be taken to rein in the misuse of power by prosecutors and hold them accountable for their actions. Prosecutorial abuse and lack of accountability affects all of us in one way or another.

(Thanks to Pastor Stuart Briscoe for outlining the questions to ask when reading the Bible: What? – does it say, So What? – what does it mean, Now What? – how does it apply to me and what action do I need to take.)

Notes in the back of each chapter cite my sources and provide further insight.

The **bibliography** provides resources written by people who confirmed what I experienced and the conclusions that I reached. These books contain so much excellent information about our justice system and how it has gone wrong.

The same can be said for the countless bits of information and stories found online of other innocent people who were charged and often convicted of crimes. I also heard personal stories from people here in Wisconsin who had similar experiences with a prosecutor.

You will notice that I include many quotes from other sources. I am doing this for two reasons: others often say something better than I can, or quotes from outside sources provide you with the fact that many others have experienced prosecutor misconduct and/or have spoken out and are demanding change. There are numerous books, articles, online publications, and reports on the devastation in the lives of so many by prosecutors with an agenda other than justice and the truth.

Prosecutor misconduct—the use and abuse of citizens—cuts across all political, socio-economic, religious, gender, and racial lines. Now, please join me in my walk through the Waukesha County Wisconsin Department of Justice and the criminal justice system.

> *"The creation of new crimes thousands of them that do not prohibit inherently wrongful conduct but, rather, punish what the average American would think of as unavoidable accidents, innocent mistakes, and other inadvertences."*
>
> *One Nation Under Arrest*, edited by Paul Rosenzweig & Brian W. Wal

Chapter 1

I'm A Criminal?

Wisconsin State Statute 939.12:

Crime defined

A crime is conduct which is prohibited by state law and punishable by fine or imprisonment or both.

The first order of business is to confirm that Grandma is NOT a criminal. Officially, I have been signed, sealed, and delivered—legally—as not being a criminal. According to the Wisconsin State statutes, I was never a criminal.

Yet a Waukesha County, Wisconsin prosecutor filed criminal charges against me twice with the full approval to do so by the district attorney of Waukesha County in 2014.

The title of this book came from the question one of our eight grandchildren asked his dad. The thirteen-year-old had been doing an assignment on the computer for a class when he ran into the mainstream media's portrayal of me, his grandmother, as being guilty of a crime.

Although I wasn't guilty, the media made it appear I was by their choice of words, misinformation, non-factual information, and slanted viewpoints. Both charges were dismissed by two different Waukesha County judges as having no probable cause. That means that there was not a legal reason for ever having issued those charges in the first place.

My beliefs about the law, about prosecutors, about crime, about my country, about equal treatment under the law, about justice, about fairness, and any other naïve fantasy about the law in our country was destroyed. I learned, personally, what the Department of Justice had become as opposed to what it was meant to be for the protection of the citizenry. I discovered that prosecutors had the dominant influence in the criminal justice system.

Although I sincerely believe that not all prosecutors are willing to commit misconduct in the abuse and use of innocent people, from almost five years of research I concluded that far too many of them are.

Although my story involves my firearm, what I found in five years of research into prosecutor misconduct is that:

> *"No one is really safe from grave injustice committed under the banner of the criminal justice system."*
>
> *One Nation Under Arrest*, edited by Paul Rosenzweig & Brian W. Walsh

Why Did Granny Get a Gun?

I decided to get my concealed carry license shortly after the Azana Spa shooting in Brookfield, Wisconsin. Some may remember the Azana Spa event. As reported in the local newspaper:

> Brookfield police reports say the Sunday morning of the mass shooting, Haughton took a cab to the salon. He was confronted by his wife Zina, who worked there. She spoke calmly to him, telling him it was a peaceful place. Witnesses say Haughton came in with a crazed look on his face, grabbed Zina by the hair and fired four shots into the ground.
>
> The third person shot…extended an arm toward Haughton and tried to reason with him.

It is believed the final shots were those that killed Zina.[1]

At that time, I distinctly remembered thinking that if a woman with the means and ability to save lives, i.e., concealed carry, was at the spa at that time, how many lives would have been saved? (Not only that, but the trauma caused to the ones who lived may have been avoided or lessened as well. I met one of those women some months ago. Talking to this beautiful young woman, who had been shot but lived, made my decision to keep training and learning just in case.)

After the thought about lives that could have been saved, I pictured myself in a restaurant or other public place with my grandchildren and a person coming in intent on murder. I thought about being unable to protect my grandchildren, to not have a chance to save their young lives.

Since I had only fired a gun once before, I immediately took classes and joined a group of women who practiced once a month at a local indoor range.

I suppose I could hope that someone else would be a concealed carry person and could save lives, including the lives of my loved ones. But as Brian Zalewski, a trainer for Applied Tactical Training Academy, said in a class that I attended: "Hope is not a good plan." Brian was one of the police officers who answered the call for help at the Azana Spa shooting.

I suppose I could only go to places that were posted *No Guns Allowed* and believe that an active shooter intent on murder would obey the signs. Concealed carry people will obey the sign and not bring a firearm inside. I certainly do.

"According to the Crime Prevention Research Center, 'gun free zones' (areas where guns are prohibited) have been the target of more than 98% of all mass shootings. This staggering number is why such designated

Attorneys for Freedom

When a *No Guns Allowed* sign is posted on the door of a building, the chances of that building being chosen by a mass murderer is substantially increased. Needless to say, the lives of the people in that building are also at more risk.[3,4]

I remembered reading about a woman who left her firearm in her car due to the *No Guns Allowed* sign on a restaurant door. A man, obviously intent on murdering as many people as he could, walked into the restaurant and started indiscriminately shooting people. This woman watched her mother and father shot to death by this man as she stood by helplessly, unable to fight back and protect them and others. Along with grieving for her mother and father, she couldn't stop thinking that they might still be alive if she had her gun and had a chance to protect lives.

I never wanted to know that I could have saved lives and didn't.

Unintentional Does Happen

March 19, 2014. I had been attending a women's Bible study at our church for many years. This day was typical of many.

We would start in the chapel for a speaker on the topic or the book of the Bible we had been studying. Then we would break into our small groups in separate rooms to review and discuss the day's lesson.

What I did that morning before study I couldn't say. As is true for many of us, there are things we do by habit or by rote because we've done it so many times.

One of those habits that I had performed for two years was to clip my Ruger .380 LCP inside my waistband. I also had the habit of taking it off in a public bathroom, putting it on the sanitary napkin disposal and then clipping back on my waistband before I left the stall. One of the reasons was the comfort. The other reason was that if I was wearing pants and, of course, pulled them down, the top of the gun was visible to whoever was in the next stall. One never knows who is next to you and what their reaction might be.

I had been in hundreds of public bathrooms over the two-year period that I carried that firearm. The habit I had established had never failed.

That day it did.

I have no idea why. Was I distracted? Was I lost in my thoughts? I'm not sure. I had been distracted or lost in thoughts many times before, but the bathroom habit I had with my gun was firm. Not that day.

What I clearly remembered about that day was that the large area by the door through which I normally exited the church was almost empty. That area was usually filled with people, the majority being women and children.

I remembered it because, on my way to the restroom, I could see one of the leaders of the women's study standing there and I waved at her. Typically, she would have been talking with a group of women. That day she was standing alone. I realized that I was leaving much later than usual.

After waving to her, I turned, went to the bathroom and after that, I left. She was the person who later went into the bathroom and found my firearm.

I went to the drive-thru at McDonald's and then drove a few blocks to a shoe store. When I sat down in the store, I realized that I didn't have my gun.

What happened when I discovered the missing firearm was so clear in my mind even now because the gut-wrenching, sick feeling I felt was severe.

I went to my car and called the church. I still remember my hand shaking as I used my finger to locate the number to the church in my contact list on my cell. The person who picked up told me that they'd found my gun and called the police, and the responding officer was currently at the church to retrieve the firearm. He would be calling me soon.

Later, when asked how much time had elapsed between leaving the church and discovering that my Ruger was missing, I figured that it had to be twenty to thirty minutes. Just to be sure, I calculated distances, and my estimated time fit. The distance to the McDonald's from the church is 1.4 miles and the distance from McDonald's to the shoe store is 1.6 miles. I got a close parking place, walked into the store, and sat down—and that's when I noticed my gun wasn't on my waist.

According to witnesses, my gun was in the bathroom less than five minutes. The timing seems to fit. In that amount of time, the police had been called; an officer had driven to the church, questioned witnesses, and had left. The police station is 5.5 miles from the church.

Knowing that my firearm was safe with the police officer, and anticipating the officer's call, I continued driving to my next appointment. The appointment was in regard to my father who was in assisted living, and I couldn't miss that appointment. I was deeply upset with myself, but I remember talking to myself to stay calm and concentrate on my driving.

The officer called me.

When the officer called, I was still crying. I don't often cry, so when I do, it must be something uniquely upsetting. I told the officer that I couldn't believe that I had done what I did—forgetting to clip my firearm back inside my waistband. That appeared in his written report. Of course, I meant that it was unusual for me to have not clipped that firearm back onto my waistband. It's hard to believe that the officer didn't understand what I meant. However, when a prosecutor with an agenda wants to twist a statement of regret into something sinister, he or she can. That is exactly what the prosecutor did.

The officer was kind and professional. He told me to go to the police station and pick up my firearm the next day. He didn't act or talk as if this was anything unusual or any big deal—and actually, that fit with what I had learned later about me being far from the only person who has forgotten a firearm in a public place, especially a bathroom.

That instruction was in line with the Wisconsin State statutes, as I learned later. The written law clearly stated that there was not a crime committed:

Wisconsin State Statute 948.55 – The Law as Written

Leaving or storing a loaded firearm within the reach or easy access of a child.

(1) In this section, "child" means a person who has not attained the age of 14 years.

(2) Whoever recklessly stores or leaves a loaded firearm within the reach or easy access of a child is guilty of a Class A misdemeanor if all of the following occur:

(a) A child obtains the firearm without the lawful permission of his or her parent or guardian or the person having charge of the child.

(b) The child under par. (a) **discharges the firearm and the discharge causes bodily harm or death to himself, herself or another.**

Nothing that would have warranted a criminal charge occurred

What is Legal and Constitutional Has Become Irrelevant

March 20, 2014. I went to the police station, as instructed by the officer, to pick up my firearm. When I told the officer at the desk my name and why I was there, he called another officer. When that officer—a lieutenant—arrived, I asked for my firearm. He looked sternly at me and told me that I would not be getting it back.

Of course, at that time, I had no idea that my United States constitutional right of due process was being violated. I had not been charged with a crime. Therefore, my personal property could not be seized. The right of due process was established by the Fourth, Fifth, and Fourteenth Amendments to the Constitution (i.e., the Bill of Rights).

Aspects of Due Process ("Fundamental Fairness")

The government must provide notice of the charges against you. *(There were not any charges against me.)*

The government must be able to show that there is an articulated (non-vague) standard of conduct which you are accused of violating. *(There was not a written law that had been violated.)*

The government must provide you with an opportunity to rebut their charges against you in a meaningful way and at a meaningful time. *(The "hearing requirement.")*

To sustain its position for the deprivation of your liberty or property, the government must establish—at a minimum—that there is substantial and credible evidence supporting its charges. *(There was not nor was there ever any evidence that a crime had been committed, yet my personal property was taken and criminal charges were issued.)*

The government must provide some explanation to the individual for the basis of any adverse finding. *(There was not nor was there ever any adverse findings.)*[5]

None of those aspects of due process had been given to me before my personal property was taken and held. There was no articulated (non-vague) standard of conduct which I was accused of violating. It wasn't until after I read my attorney's defense against the criminal charge made against me and after I began to research prosecutor misconduct that all the pieces of what had happened came together.

It was in my attorney's written defense that I learned the reality of what the Fourth, Fifth, and Fourteenth Amendments personally meant to me as a citizen of the United States of America. The Bill of Rights was written to protect me and all citizens against a government that could do whatever it wanted to do.

In my personal experience and in my research, I realized that the keeping of personal property without due process had become a common and unchallenged practice. I doubt that many police officers or prosecutors even give it a second thought. Not only that, but when personal property is taken without due process, it requires hiring an attorney and going to court to get it back.

As my reality took hold, I realized that my property and liberty could be taken from me, taken from any citizen of this country, without any legal reason. Liberty and personal property could be taken for totally arbitrary reasons.

In Chapter 2, I meet with the prosecutor for a "pre-charge" interview.

"Injustice anywhere is a threat to justice everywhere."

Martin Luther King, Jr.

Notes Chapter 1

1   Katie Delong, "October 21st Marks Three-year Anniversary of Shooting at Azana Salon & Spa in Brookfield," FOX6Now.com, October 21, 2015, https://fox6now.com/2015/10/21/october-21st-marks-three-year-anniversary-of-shooting-at-azana-salon-spa-in-brookfield/.
2   The study covers 1950 through May 2018.
3   John Fund, "The Facts about Mass Shootings," *National Review*, December 16, 2012, https://www.nationalreview.com/2012/12/facts-about-mass-shootings-john-fund/.
4   Massad Ayoob, "The False Hope of Gun-Free Zones," American Handgunner, https://americanhandgunner.com/the-ayoob-files/the-false-hope-of-gun-free-zones/.

"Gun-free zones have been the most popular response to previous mass killings. But many law-enforcement officials say they are actually counterproductive. "Guns are already banned in schools. That is why the shootings happen in schools. A school is a 'helpless-victim zone,'" says Richard Mack, a former Arizona sheriff. "Preventing any adult at a school from having access to a firearm eliminates any chance the killer can be stopped in time to prevent a rampage," ("The Magic of Gun Control" Sheriff Richard Mack)

"Jim Kouri, the public-information officer of the National Association of Chiefs of Police noted that the Aurora shooter, who killed twelve people earlier this year, had a choice of seven movie theaters that were showing the Batman movie he was obsessed with. All were within a 20-minute drive of his home. The Cinemark Theater the killer ultimately chose wasn't the closest, but it was the only one that posted signs saying it banned concealed handguns carried by law-abiding individuals.

Disarming law-abiding citizens leaves them as sitting ducks. A couple hundred people were in the Cinemark Theater when the killer arrived. There is an extremely high probability that one or more of them would have had a legal concealed handgun with him if they had not been banned." (National Review)

5   Doug Linder, "Procedural Due Process: What Individual Interests Are Protected? What Process Must Government Provide?" http://law2.umke.edu/faculty/projects/ftrails/conlaw/proseduraldueprocess.html

On Occasion, when speaking to a group about my experience and my research on prosecutor misconduct someone will ask why I had a gun in church. Churches are not immune from mass shootings. In fact:

> *"CHURCH SHOOTINGS HAPPEN OFTEN ENOUGH THAT THERE'S A NATIONAL CHURCH SHOOTING DATABASE A dig into the data reveals that not all of them are motivated by prejudice, but a significant portion are."* (Pacific Standard)

> "SCOTTS, Mich. (RNS) — *"Did they know how many rounds a gunman fired into First Baptist Church in Sutherland Springs, Texas?*
>
> *Did they know how many little boys and girls he killed?*
>
> *Did they know there was a second violent church attack that same day in Fresno, Calif.?*
>
> *Barry Young's voice rose as he led an "intruder awareness and response training" for church personnel this month at Prairie Baptist Church in Scotts, Mich.*
>
> *"We've got to get church leaders' heads out of the sand."* (USA Today)

For more information on this topic, email: Susan@ GoToJustGrandma.com or go to my website: www. GoToJustGrandma.com/contact and request the chapter, not in this book, **Freedom, Fear Fanning, Faith and Firearms**

Who are the most common targets for prosecutors willing to

use innocent people for their own personal, professional, and/
or political purposes?

My almost 5-year study of prosecutor misconduct revealed
that the politically incorrect or those that worked for politically
incorrect companies were prosecutor targets. In these cases,
it was often vague laws that were used, made-up, fabricated
crimes, or no crime at all. The majority of these people where
Caucasian.

My book focuses on what is most familiar to me and that with
which I can identify.

However, there are other "groups" of people who are targeted.
The Innocent Project's statistics show that the majority of
convicted yet innocent people are black males. Most of these
crimes are murder, rape, robbery.

Statistics from the Innocence Project:

Races of the 353 exonerees

   219 African Americans, 106 Caucasians, 26 Latinos, 2
   Asian American

Three of the books in my bibliography cover this and there
are more:

   Davis, A.J. (2007). <u>Arbitrary Justice: The Power of The
   American Prosecutor</u>

   Butler, Paul (2009), <u>Let's Get Free: A Hip-Hop Theory of
   Justice</u>

   Natapoff, Alexandra (2018) <u>Punishment Without Crime</u>

Chapter 2

Enter the Prosecutor

Although this is my story, let me emphasize that many, many other people have experienced exactly what I did at the hands of a prosecutor. Or, they experienced other forms of a prosecutor using an innocent person for that prosecutor's personal, professional, and/ or political agenda.

Obviously, I must use the people involved in my case. Please know this is not just about these prosecutors. It is about what they did and the fact that so many other prosecutors are doing the same things at the cost of justice, freedom, liberty, and the pursuit of happiness for numerous innocent people.

Keeping a Timeline

It was a while before I started keeping a timeline of events (see timeline at the end of this Chapter). I don't know exactly when the prosecutor called me to set up a pre-charge interview.

How did the Waukesha County Department of Justice hear about this incident in the first place? The official police report said that it was referred to the Waukesha County District Attorney Office for general review. I don't know if the prosecutor called the police station and told the lieutenant not to return my personal property.[1]

The responding officer who called me, after he had interviewed witnesses at the church, told me to do what was constitutionally correct: go to the station and pick up my firearm. Therefore, that may have been what this police department usually did in a case like this. The law specifically stated that no crime had been committed.

The local mainstream media had already started reporting on this before any charges were made, taking pictures of the church and attempting to interview women who attended the morning Bible study. I was embarrassed for what, although unintentionally, I caused for the church I had attended for over thirty years. At this point, because there had been no criminal charges, the media did not release my name. That would come later and would compound every one of those feelings.

I was experiencing many upsetting emotions. I felt guilty—even though I did not do this purposely—embarrassed, anxious, confused, and helpless. I was only sleeping with the help of a mild tranquilizer prescribed by my doctor. From reading accounts of other innocent people who have experienced being charged with a crime by a prosecutor who had a reason other than the law to issue criminal charges, I had learned that these pervasive and painful negative emotions were essentially the same.

The Pre-Charge Meeting with the Prosecutor

April 11, 2014. What registered with me immediately is how the prosecutor walked into the room where I had been taken, and even before she shut the door, she started talking: "I was going to charge you with a crime, but now, I'm not sure."

I cannot totally describe this room except to say that it appeared to be a small room for holding meetings. I remember sitting across from her at a table. But even after five years, I am certain that those were her exact words. Not only did I remember that scene, but I had written everything down within minutes of the interview.

I was shocked because, by then, I had read the Wisconsin State statutes and, according to the law written by the Legislative Branch of government, I knew I had not committed a crime.

Wisconsin State Statues clearly states that unless the firearm is picked up by a child (under 14) without parental permission and that the child discharges the gun and injures himself or another, there is not a crime.

Wisconsin State Statute 948.55

Leaving or storing a loaded firearm within the reach or easy access of a child

All of the following needs to occur in order to have the facts that would establish probable cause to issue a criminal charge:

- A child obtains the firearm without lawful permission from parent or guardian
- The child discharges the firearm and the discharge causes bodily harm or death to himself, herself or another.

At that time, I believed that the job of the Judicial Branch of government was to interpret and enforce the law. It was years of research that proved to me how very wrong I was.

The prosecutor and I talked for about twenty minutes. During the entire time, I registered my sorrow and regret. I added that I couldn't believe that I had done what I did. I had been in bathrooms hundreds of times and never forgot to put my firearm back where it belonged. I told her that I had been a vigilant firearm user and concealed carry person. I just couldn't understand how I forgot; it was so unlike me. I also told her that I had talked to experienced instructors about how to best deal with my gun when in the bathroom and planned to follow their advice.

Early in the interview, the prosecutor said something to the effect that under different circumstances, she and I could be friends. I registered this as a strange comment but didn't fixate on it. After that, she asked me if I had an attorney. I did not, because, in my naiveté, I didn't think I needed one—I hadn't committed a crime. Then the prosecutor told me that she had planned to charge me with reckless endangerment but now she was undecided. My heart stopped, the tears started, and I felt pure panic.

I told her that I had read the Wisconsin State statutes. Wisconsin State Statute 948.55 fit perfectly with what I did. That statute also clearly delineated under what conditions my actions *would* be a crime. Because none of those elements of a crime were present, I knew I had not committed a crime according to the written law.

She replied that there were "other things" to charge me with.

Since she mentioned the media several times during that interview, I started to think that because the media had blown this up, she felt she must appease the media by charging me.

I said to her, regarding her comments about the media, that I was the trifecta of the kind of people the media loved to demonize. I was a Caucasian, Christian, conservative. Added to that a Second Amendment supporter who had concealed carry. I wondered if it was because of the media that she was planning to charge me with a crime regardless. She assured me that this wasn't true.

I said, "Tell me that if this had happened in another place and not a Christian church and by a person *different* than what I am, that this would have made the news at all?"

She didn't answer me.

"Further, to be faithful to their principals' interests, prosecutors have an incentive to discriminate against particular defendants or subgroups of defendants by attempting to settle like cases differently depending on defendants' personal characteristics unrelated to culpability."

Jeffrey Standen, "Plea Bargaining in
the Shadow of the Guidelines"

Then, the prosecutor told me it would take her months to decide whether to charge me with a crime. I later learned this was a violation of her duty as a prosecutor.[2]

I broke down. I started thinking about my grandkids walking into school and being kidded about their grandmother, the criminal. And, I had to wait for months to even know if this would be my fate.

Then, paradoxically, she said, "I don't want to have you wait." She told me she would decide by Friday. I countered that I better hire a lawyer and start preparing my family for what they would have to deal with.

She told me what could happen if I were charged: jail, a considerable fine, and so on. Then when my mouth fell open, and the tears kept coming, she quickly said that she didn't think that I would go to jail.

She then mentioned that she had spoken to the district attorney (DA) about this case. With similar cases, he just had the person take a gun safety class. When she asked if I had ever had one, I told her about practicing at least once a month—most of the time with experienced instructors helping us—and when she asked me if I would be willing to take another gun safety class, I told her that I would, of course. (I went home and signed up for one. I had already taken several, but I wanted to make sure I was doing everything I could.)

Before our meeting was over, I stated that I should probably get an attorney right away. She said that was my right, but encouraged me to wait until she decided, by Friday, whether she was going to charge me: "Why don't you wait to hire an attorney until I decide?"

Then she said, "Now don't let this define you."

As I stood up and was ready to leave, she remarked, "Well, the media got this."

Something Isn't Right

After that interview, something didn't feel right. Although I was severely shaken by the entire meeting, my gut signaled that I had better write the whole thing down immediately. I started writing on the way home while my husband drove. As soon as we got back, I typed it and saved it to my computer.

There is the old saying that hindsight is 20/20. Often when we look back at an incident with new information, a different attitude, and/or personal growth, we see and understand things differently.

During these years since that interview I have learned so much about the law, the Bill of Rights, the Biblical foundation of our law, the rule of law, ethical standards for prosecutors, and the ever-increasing abuse of all of it. The growing misuse of absolute power by the criminal justice system came alive for me with the many examples of the innocent people whose lives had been shattered— shattered by a justice system that grants tyrannical power to its prosecutors with no consequences to the prosecutor regardless of the damage they cause to their fellow human beings.[3]

Since that day in 2014, I have read all or parts of over twenty books on the subject. I have a computer full of research, examples of misconduct and prosecutorial abuse, legal terms, laws, statutes, legal articles dating back decades and to the present on the danger of the absolute power given to the American prosecutor and suggestions for reform. I've shared some of the best of these in the Bibliography.

When I am searching any subject, my goal is to look at the facts. That is what provides the preponderance of evidence for truth. As I researched and studied, it became evident to me that what I had experienced was wrong—legally, morally, ethically. And it was happening to many, many citizens not only in Wisconsin and Waukesha County but in every state and every county and city in this entire country.

With that in mind, let me present to you the insights about that interview that came to light for me as I reviewed that interview throughout these past years.

Developing 20/20 Hindsight

One of the first statements that the prosecutor made to me was "under different circumstances, we could be friends." That made me feel uncomfortable. In fact, it made me feel creepy. She had been talking to me for just a short period of time when she said that.

Imagine a police officer, male or female, stopping you for speeding and while writing the ticket said something like that -"Under different circumstances, we could be friends." Or the IRS agent, male or female, who called you in for an audit saying, after talking with you for about five minutes- "Under different circumstances, we could be friends."

Would your mind go to manipulation of some kind or a "come on"?

That statement gave me a gut feeling that I had better write down what happened in that interview. It struck me, even then, as being bizarre and highly inappropriate.

With new knowledge and going back to that interview, I saw what certainly appears to have been the manipulative tactics that the prosecutor used to discourage me from hiring an attorney before she could officially make the first charge.

Why didn't I hire an attorney immediately after that interview? I was not only inexperienced with the criminal court system, but I was an emotional mess. That, of course, made me vulnerable to wanting to believe what I was being led to believe. In my opinion, I think that the prosecutor led me to believe that not hiring an attorney before she decided was in my best interest. She even requested "Why don't you wait." Since the law stated that I hadn't committed a crime, I foolishly believed that she didn't want me to spend money unnecessarily because she had no plans to charge me.

I was a sixty-six-year-old woman who had no experience with the criminal justice system. Of course, I believed that she was not going to charge me with a crime. I really thought she was doing her job but cared about this terrified, tearful, repentant senior citizen. I later came to realize that she advised me to wait on hiring an attorney so she could have the upper hand in prosecuting me.

Now, knowing what I know, I should have walked right out of there and hired an attorney. That may have been the only thing that would have stopped that first "no legal reason" charge right there.

Government Chick's Tricks on Gullible Granny TIC (Totally Insignificant Citizen)[4,5]

It was only later, with 20/20 hindsight loaded with new information, that I finally saw the whole combination of (what certainly appears to be) tactics employed by the prosecutor to manipulate me from hiring an attorney. She was following her plan from the very beginning—the "pre-charge" interview. I don't think she wanted an attorney having any part in her "decision process."

First: Scaring me—she walked in saying she planned to charge me with a crime.

Next: Saying that now she wasn't sure—ah—she gave me hope.

Then: She implies that she is my friend—see, she is telling me, "You can trust me."

However: The prosecutor reminds me that she is in control of how long I stay anxious over her decision and tells me it will take months to decide if she is going to charge me with a crime.

But wait: She promises that she will decide my fate by Friday— wow, the prosecutor really is my friend, she is doing this just for me. What a wonderful person!

But then: She tells me that I could be charged a huge fine and even go to jail.

And, just in time, the caring "friend" returns: She tells me she is sure I won't go to jail and then tells me that the district attorney with a similar case only had the person take a gun safety class and would I do that. Hope again! She will save me from jail, and her example of what to do in this case is her boss, the DA, I was to believe that, of course, she would do what her boss did.

Then: I finally wisely say, "I better get an attorney right away."

Legally: She must tell me that it is my right to get an attorney.

Back again is my caring "friend" who returned after telling me that I might go to jail: She kindly said to me: "Why don't you wait to get an attorney until I decide."

I hear: "Of course, I, the prosecutor, will do what my boss the district attorney did—I'll just have you take a gun safety course. So, don't waste your money hiring an attorney."

With 20/20 hindsight, now I know that I should have never walked into that room without an attorney in the first place. Knowing that Wisconsin State statutes clearly stated that no crime was committed yet being told I might be charged with a crime; I should have asked for an attorney right then and there.

This Waukesha County prosecutor knew who she had sitting in front of her: a person completely inexperienced in the criminal justice system. Now, with 20/20 hindsight and new information it is hard for me to deny that this wasn't manipulation. I took the bait—hook, line, and sinker.

Perhaps it seems hard to believe that any intelligent person could be so easily misled. All I can say is that no one can know what this experience is like without experiencing it.

Was the Prosecutor Planning to Charge Me
with a Crime before She Ever Met Me?

I concluded that she, indeed, had planned to charge me with a crime before she even met me. However, I think that she needed to interview me for two reasons: First, she wanted to ascertain whether I had an attorney, and second, to observe my state of mind to see how easy I would fold when criminally charged.

Both of those goals were quickly met. I didn't have an attorney. When told that there were "other things" to charge me with, my panicked look was unmistakable. And, when she had told me what could happen, jail, a considerable fine, etc., my mouth fell open, and the tears started. She then knew my state of mind: weak, vulnerable, and criminal court clueless.

This prosecutor knew that she had a frightened, anxious person and that the chances that I would quickly give in and admit to a crime when I never committed one were extremely high. She would have her win, and that was that.

It was much later that I realized winning was valued in the criminal justice system. Winning meant getting a conviction regardless of how it was gotten. Winning also meant, as I discovered later, issuing a charge without a legal reason and testing the system to see if a conviction would result.

The fact that the media played a huge part in her decision to charge me criminally was obvious. She often mentioned it during the interview. Her last words to me were: "Well, the media got this."

The clincher for me that she had decided to charge me with a crime before she ever met me was this statement: "Now don't let this define you."

I never saw the implication of that statement until just a few months after I started writing this book. Only an official criminal charge could define me, therefore, the prosecutor had to have known what she was always going to do.

After looking at that interview with new knowledge, it is hard for me to believe that she had not made the decision to charge me as a criminal as soon as the "media got this." The media was already all over this case, even before I was charged. That would make it easier for her to get a win.

My unintentional act had, without a doubt, emotionally impacted me severely, but I would eventually get over the pain and retain the lesson learned. (In fact, in the now total of eight years that I have been carrying a firearm, forgetting it in a public place had never happened before that one time and has not happened since.)

However, if she charged me with a crime, the media could now use my name. I would then be defined as "a criminal." Regardless of innocence or guilt, most people decide that someone is guilty of a crime the moment the media reports it. Any prosecutor certainly knows that. This prosecutor knew what would happen to me the minute my name was released. That was why the comment: "Now don't let this define you." It did define me, of course.

Did the prosecutor make that comment to assuage any guilt she might have, a moment of human compassion? I have no idea.

The qualities of a good prosecutor are as elusive and as impossible to define as those which mark a gentleman. And those who need to be told would not understand it anyway. A sensitiveness to fair play and sportsmanship is perhaps the best protection against the abuse of power, and the citizen's safety lies in the prosecutor who tempers zeal with human kindness, who seeks truth and not victims, who serves the law and not factional purposes, and who approaches his task with humility.

Edited by Timothy Lynch, *In The Name of Justice: Leading Experts Reexamine the Classic Article "The Aims of Criminal Law*

The Prosecutor "Officially" Decides My Fate

April 16, 2014. The prosecutor called and left a message on my phone that she was charging me with negligent handling of a weapon: Wisconsin State Statute 941.20(1)(a). She stated that she was asking for a fine and the forfeiture of my firearm.

Wisconsin State Statute 941.20(1)(a)

Endangering safety by use of dangerous weapon

Endangers another's safety by the negligent operation or handling of a dangerous weapon

Obviously, the prosecutor could not charge me with the only Wisconsin State Statute that perfectly described what happened because that Statute perfectly stated that there was not a crime committed.

Wisconsin State Statute 948.55

Leaving or storing a loaded firearm within the reach or easy access of a child

All of the following needs to occur in order to have the facts that would establish probable cause to issue a criminal charge:

- A child obtains the firearm without lawful permission from parent or guardian
- The child discharges the firearm and the discharge causes bodily harm or death to himself, herself or another.

None of the above happened—thank God. My firearm was in the bathroom for less than five minutes, picked up by an adult, given to another adult. There were no children anywhere in the area.

The prosecutor knew that Statute existed. Remember that I quoted it to her and stated that I knew that a crime had not been committed according to the law. Her reply was that there were "other things she could charge me with."

In the message that the prosecutor left on my phone, she stated that she needed to "send a message to the community." I recorded her message and saved it to my computer.

At that time, I didn't understand probable cause. I didn't know about the ethical rule for prosecutors written by the Wisconsin Supreme Court. As my research continued and as I became more familiar with "legal" language, I began to understand more about what is going wrong in our criminal justice system.

But, now, I needed to hire an attorney.

"In matters of truth and justice, there is no difference between large and small problems, for issues concerning the treatment of people are all the same."

Albert Einstein

1 Later, after the first charge (negligent handling of a weapon: Wisconsin Statute 941.20(1)(a)) had been dismissed as having no probable cause, I learned that the prosecutor *did* instruct the lieutenant in Brookfield, WI to refuse to return my personal property. I had no criminal charges or convictions against me after the dismissal of that first charge. Therefore, there was no legal reason not to return my firearm. According to the Fourth, Fifth, and Fourteenth Amendments, in instructing the lieutenant not to return my firearm, the prosecutor violated my constitutional rights.

2 The American Bar Association, "Criminal Justice Standards for the Prosecution Function," https://www. americanbar.org/groups/criminal_justice/standards/ ProsecutionFunctionFourthEdition/
Standard 3-1.9 Diligence, Promptness and Punctuality:
(a) "The prosecutor should act with diligence and promptness to investigate, litigate, and dispose of criminal charges, consistent with the interests of justice and with due regard for fairness, accuracy, and rights of the defendant, victims, and witnesses.
(b) "The prosecutor should use procedures that will cause delay only when there is a legitimate basis for such use, and not to secure an unfair tactical advantage."

3 It is in those sources that I read some of the details of the collateral damage done by the false criminal charges of rogue prosecutors. Lives shattered? I read of two suicides. Many of the victims lost their entire life savings; many innocent people spent years and even decades in jail. I read of those who suffered mental breakdowns. One counselor compared the emotional damage to be much like PTSD. I understand this, because I experienced it. This ordeal was difficult and life-altering. Yet, it also provided me with the opportunity to be one more voice in exposing the ongoing threat to our

freedom. An arbitrary, all-powerful group of government employees with fundamentally no accountability is a danger to the safety and well-being of all of us.

4   These people are "average" citizens who I sometimes have referred to as TICs (Totally Insignificant Citizens). TICs appear to be considered "usable sources" for the prosecutor's own purposes. After reading and learning about so many "average" citizens who were misused by prosecutors, it seemed to me as if we are viewed as inanimate pieces on a game board to be played to establish a "win" for the prosecutor.

5   The Crime Report, "Inconvenient Truths: Why False Confessions Still Warp U.S. Justice," May 23, 2019, https:// thecrimereport.org/2019/05/23/inconvenient-truths-why-false-confessions-still-warp-us-justice/

Timeline of Grandma's Case

March 19, 2014: I forget my firearm in a public restroom.

April 11, 2014: "Pre-charge" meeting with the State of Wisconsin prosecutor.

April 16, 2014: The prosecutor calls and leaves a message on my phone that she is charging me with negligent handling of a weapon: Wisconsin State Statute 941.20(1)(a), Endangering safety by use of dangerous weapon. She says she's asking for a fine and the forfeiture of my firearm.

April 18, 2014: I meet with an attorney.

May 5, 2014: Initial court appearance with the court commissioner.

June 9, 2014: Hon. Judge Lloyd V. Carter takes the case "under advisement."

June 19, 2014: Case dismissed due to no probable cause.

August 18, 2014: Phone contact with the lieutenant at Town of Brookfield Police Department concerning the return of personal property seized/kept without due process of law. The state prosecutor instructs the lieutenant to keep personal property—in violation of the Fourth, Fifth, and Fourteenth Amendments to the United States Constitution and in violation of Article I, Section 11 of the Wisconsin Constitution.

September 14, 2014: The prosecutor threatens, via my attorney, to issue another criminal charge unless I accept a more severe punishment (plea bargain).

September 23, 2014: My husband asks me to offer something in lieu of accepting the plea bargain, in order to alleviate the stress of this situation on my physical and emotional health. Offer made, offer rescinded within days.

October 8, 2014: My defense attorney reports no contact from the prosecutor.

November 25, 2014: Two months later, the prosecutor threatens to charge me with another crime unless her terms are accepted. I refuse her terms.

November 27, 2014: The prosecutor issues a second criminal charge of criminal disorderly conduct (Wisconsin State Statute 947.01).

November 27, 2014: Wisconsin Carry issues a statement condemning the actions of the Waukesha County DA's office.

December 3, 2014: Wisconsin Carry informs me that they have received hundreds of responses from people supporting the condemnation of the prosecutor's actions. I also learn that many people contacted the district attorney's (DA's) office agreeing with the condemnation of the prosecutor's actions.

December 7, 2014: The prosecutor makes a "kinder, gentler" offer (less of a fine and less time without my Second Amendment rights). I refuse her terms.

December 8, 2014: Second time in court. As I did last time, I signed an Authorization to Appear statement that I would not have to appear in court. This time I decided that I would appear in court.

March 3, 2015: I appeared in court before Hon. Judge Lee S. Dreyfus, Jr. with my attorney and approximately a dozen supporters. Judge set the date of March 31 to verbally announce his decision.

March 31, 2015: I appeared with my attorney and some supporters. Judge Dreyfus agreed with Judge Carter's decision, saying: (1) no charges are necessary, (2) this was not intentional on the defendant's part—may have been negligent but not to the point of criminal, therefore no probable cause, (3) the law is made by the legislature, not by the justice branch of government; therefore, case dismissed for the second time. In both criminal charges, the prosecutor did not have a probable cause, i.e., no legal reason for a criminal charge.

Chapter 3

Hiring a Defense Attorney

On what basis does someone, who has never committed a crime (and according to the law as written, still hadn't), hire a defense attorney?

I started a search on my computer.

A name popped up: Attorney Tom Grieve. I called him and made an appointment for April 18, 2014. Of course, I was praying for guidance. What is incredible is that I had no idea how that pop-up popped up. I could never get it to happen again doing what I did before.

Am I saying that was answered prayer? I am. Now, some of you are out there nodding in agreement, maybe even a few Amens! And some of you have those little smirky smiles forming on your faces 😊.

Attorney Grieve was an excellent choice for me. He was sincere and caring in that first interview and continued to be so throughout the whole process. I was such an emotional wreck when I went to see him that I could barely talk through the tears. He was kind and understanding and very quickly filed a defense against that first charge.

I had told him that I had written down all that happened in the pre-charge interview immediately after it was over. Attorney Grieve asked me to email him a copy and I did.

It took me a year or so after the second charge was dismissed, in March 2015, to really read all the legal information received from my attorney that I had in my possession. I didn't even read most of it while all this was going on. The entire process was so emotionally disturbing that when I read anything about it, I would typically get a sinking feeling and tears in my eyes. Looking at it all objectively was impossible. That ended up being a good thing. When I finally had the emotional peace and the concentration to read the legalese, I had done enough research that it was easier for me to interpret it.

In part, Attorney Grieve's first written defense asking for the case to be dismissed read:

> ...Because the criminal complaint by which the defendant is charged is defective.
>
> Specifically, the complaint fails to set forth essential facts from which it could be inferred that the defendant committed a crime, and fails to state the essential facts constituting the offense charged as required by law, all in violation of the rights guaranteed by the 4th, 5th, and 14th Amendments to the United States Constitution; article I, sections 1, 8, and 11 of the Wisconsin Constitution; sections 968.01 and 968.02 of the Wisconsin State Statutes...

In other words, there is no legal, lawful reason for this charge. It's defective. There is no probable cause. My constitutional rights were violated.

The prosecutor's job was to file probable cause. What the prosecutor filed was merely the officer's written report from the day police were called to the church and interviewed witnesses. The officer's report did not show probable cause for a criminal charge.

Probable cause:

> Apparent facts discovered through logical inquiry that would lead a reasonable, intelligent, and prudent person to believe

that an accused person has committed a crime, thereby warranting his or her prosecution.

Probable cause is a level of reasonable belief, based on facts that can be articulated, that is required to prosecute a person in criminal court before a person can be prosecuted; the prosecutor must possess enough facts that would lead a reasonable person to believe the claim or charge is true.

The probable cause standard is more important in Criminal Law than it is in Civil Law.[1]

In fact, it seems that the only probable cause was the prosecutor's several comments in the pre-charge interview regarding "the media got this." And, her comment in her call to me, in which she said that she was charging me with a crime to "send a message to the community." Obviously, neither of these is legal probable cause to charge someone with a crime. But she did indeed charge me with a crime.

There is an ethical rule for prosecutors in the State of Wisconsin written by the Wisconsin Supreme Court. It is in the section "Rules of Professional Conduct."

SCR (Supreme Court Rule) 20:3.8

Special responsibilities of a prosecutor

(a) A prosecutor in a criminal case or a proceeding that could result in deprivation of liberty shall not prosecute a charge that the prosecutor knows is not supported by probable cause.[2]

The American Bar Association has a similar rule of conduct:

Rule 3.8

The prosecutor in a criminal case shall:

(a) refrain from prosecuting a charge that the prosecutor knows is not supported by probable cause.[3]

And on misconduct, according to the Wisconsin Supreme Court ruling:

SCR 20:8.4

Misconduct

It is professional misconduct for a lawyer to:

(a) violate or attempt to violate the Rules of Professional Conduct, knowingly assist or induce another to do so, or do so through the acts of another.[4]

Let's apply logic. The prosecutor either:

- knew she had no probable cause, which is an ethical violation, and according to the Supreme Court Rule, is misconduct.
- didn't know she didn't have probable cause, which may indicate that she doesn't know the law and may not be qualified for her job.
- was attempting to make law, which would mean that she may have been trying to legislate from the DA's office, thereby crossing the lines of the separation of powers.[5]

Remember the two elements required by written law (Wisconsin State Statute 948.55) that need to be present when a firearm is left by the owner in a public place for that to be a crime? The two elements that would make this a crime are:

1. A child under 14 picks it up
2. The child harms himself or others.

Neither of these two elements were present in my case.

As you read on, I believe that you will realize that if my case had not been dismissed by two different judges in two different charges, it could have easily set precedent for not only firearms but also other unintentional acts.

Next stop—criminal court.

Notes Chapter 3

1   "Probable cause." The Free Dictionary. https://legal-dictionary.thefreedictionary.com/probable+cause

2   SCR 20:3.8 Special responsibilities of a prosecutor. https://docs.legis.wisconsin.gov/misc/scr/20/_992?up=1

3   American Bar Association, "Rule 3.8: Special Responsibilities of a Prosecutor," https://www.americanbar.org/groups/professional_responsibility/publications/model_rules_of_professional_conduct/rule_3_8_special_responsibilities_of_a_prosecutor/

4   SCR 20:8.4 Misconduct. https://docs.legis.wisconsin.gov/misc/scr/20/_1428

5   The Founders on the separation of powers:
"The accumulation of all powers, legislative, executive, and judiciary, in the same hands, whether of one, a few, or many, and whether hereditary, self-appointed, or elective, may justly be pronounced the very definition of tyranny." – James Madison, *Federalist 47*, 1788

"An elective despotism was not the government we fought for; but one in which the powers of government should be so divided and balanced among the several bodies of magistracy as that no one could transcend their legal limits without being effectually checked and restrained by the others." – James Madison, *Federalist 84*, 1788

"It will not be denied that power is of an encroaching nature and that it ought to be effectually restrained from passing the limits assigned to it." – James Madison, *Federalist 48*, 1788

Chapter 4

What's a Nice Girl Like You
Doing in a Place Like This?[1]

May 5, 2014

Time to take a walk to criminal court with Grandma, where she has never ever been before. This court appearance was before the court commissioner.

We were in a room with the rest of the accused. At the front of that room and behind glass windows sat all the attorneys. The court commissioner sat on a bench at the front. It didn't take long for me to see that this was a well-orchestrated ritual where everyone except for me seemed to know what to do and what the probable outcome would be.

As I watched it all unfold, it appeared that the attorneys knew, the court employees knew, actual criminals knew, and the court commissioner knew what their "assigned" roles were. I had a distinct feeling that this same ritual was played out daily. It played out like a fixed routine: mechanical, habitual, rote. It was like a worn-out skit where the actors went through their ritualized roles methodically.

I wish I could accurately describe how I felt that first time I was ever in criminal court. I didn't feel like myself at all. It was almost like a disturbing dream which produces fear and anxiety, and it wouldn't end—I couldn't "wake up."

My attorney had told me that the chance of a court commissioner dismissing a case was close to never.

I was prepared. However, what I was not prepared for was the local mainstream media. I didn't know the damage that would be caused to me as a person by a group of "elitists" who appeared to not care about facts, feeling, or the fate of their intended victim.

Experiencing what the media did to me has made me look even more closely at what they report, especially about people who don't fit their narrative. Also remember that what happened to me can, and does, happen to innocent citizens throughout this country.

The Media Misleading the Public

The media had a camera and cameraman placed in front of those glass windows, I assumed to capture a picture of the most treacherous and despicable alleged criminal in that room.

I wondered who it was.

My attorney informed me that it was me.

ME!

The media was there for me?

Numerous people—all men, as far as I know—had done what I did. In fact, in many of those instances, the firearm they left behind was in a public place much longer, and there were children around. Yet, because the Wisconsin State statutes clearly stated under what circumstances that would be a crime, no one had ever been charged before.

My denial was beginning to give way to what others had been telling me. This charge was political. I really was being used for the benefit of others and their career advancements. The DA was running for Wisconsin attorney general. And, as the prosecutor said: "Well, the media got this." Doesn't this make one wonder if it is the *media* that decides who to charge with a crime, and not the Department of Justice? Caucasian, Christian, conservative, a gun left at a mega Christian church—of course the media "got" my case. I was red meat for the mainstream media. I could almost see the drool.[1] I was everything the mainstream media had their sights on to destroy and discredit.

I didn't know it then, but I was going to experience the local mainstream media's disdain for people like me up close and personal—and in ways so low that I didn't think even they would be capable of doing.

Sitting next to us in the alleged criminal part of the room was who I came to learn to be Channel 4 (NBC affiliate) reporter Jonah Kaplan. I noticed him because we had to tell him to turn off his phone as requested. He turned out to be the microcosm of the mainstream media's bias.

We were all taken into the room behind the glass to the court commissioner's bench and signed in. Then we were released back to the room on the other side of the glass. As each case was called, each alleged criminal was called in and stood in front of the court commissioner usually with an attorney.

I was called in.

Standing there with my attorney, I felt awkward and horribly uncomfortable. For one brief moment, I put my hands behind my back. In a flash, my mind said: *Would they (the media) really be that underhanded, that nasty, that dishonest?* And I quickly put my hands back in front of me.

Unbelievably, they (the media) were that underhanded, that nasty, and that dishonest:

When the picture was published, it was shown at a distance and, of course, it looks like I was handcuffed.

That was the beginning of the local mainstream media's public mind manipulation. No one there that day had handcuffs. I was never arrested. There never *were* handcuffs.

This picture still makes me sick knowing that children and adults whom I loved and loved me back as well as people who were merely acquainted with me had seen this horrible misrepresentation of my personhood. Seeing it again takes me back to all the emotional pain and sleepless nights I had experienced.

I still find it unbelievable that the Waukesha County DA, who had other cases just like mine, had never put those people through what I was going through. It still makes me sick that the prosecutor could look me in the eyes and say: "Under other circumstances, we could be friends" while she, in all probability, knew what she was going to do and what would happen to me.

As previously said, my attorney had prepared me for the fact that in this initial hearing the court commissioner rarely to never dismissed a case. He would pass it on to a judge.

Remember, with the signed approval of the DA, the prosecutor charged me with endangering safety by use of a dangerous weapon, a Class A misdemeanor under section 941.20(1)(a) of the Wisconsin State statutes:

Wisconsin State Statute 941.20(1)(a)

Endangering safety by use of dangerous weapon

Endangers another's safety by the negligent operation or handling of a dangerous weapon.

My attorney presented a defense and reason to dismiss the case. In the written request to dismiss the case he wrote:

"To endanger the safety of another means that someone must have been directly endangered by the actions of the defendant. In fact, it does not stop there. The jury instructions dwell on this fact to such a great extent that it describes the extremely high level of endangerment that must take place. Unless one adopts the premise that the weapon could act on its own, then one cannot argue that someone on the other side of the building was directly endangered in the criminal complaint."

(Factually, the children were gone at that time. Even if the gun could act on its own, it could only endanger an empty classroom.)

"Accordingly, the Defense would ask that the Court would dismiss this criminal complaint as insufficient."

My attorney was entirely and legally correct. In fact, here are the Wisconsin State statutes that define a crime and define criminal negligence:

Wisconsin State Statute 939.12

Crime defined

A crime is conduct which is prohibited by state law and punishble by fine or imprisonment or both.

Wisconsin State Statute 939.25

Criminal negligence

(1) In this section, "criminal negligence" means ordinary negligence to a high degree, consisting of conduct that the actor should realize creates a substantial and unreasonable risk of death or great bodily harm to another.

In charging me with a crime, not only did the DA and the prosecutor totally ignore the law written by the Legislative Branch of government, i.e., Wisconsin State Statute 948.55, but so did the court commissioner. In addition to ignoring the only written law that was specific to the event, the statuary definitions of crime and of criminal negligence were also ignored by all of them.

But the court commissioner said that probable cause was proved because the person who found the gun (an adult) was "carrying it around in an unsafe manner." That statement almost makes it sound as if the woman was walking around willy-nilly waving the gun around.

In her written witness report, the woman who found the firearm reported that she was carrying the gun barrel down and was holding it by the barrel, much the way we are taught to carry scissors when we walk with them. Her finger was nowhere near the trigger. In fact, she walked out of the bathroom on the way to the information desk, which is a very short distance. Before she even got there, the head of maintenance was going to his office, which is steps from that bathroom, and he took the gun from her.

In the witness report, the man who took the gun from her was asked if anyone was endangered by the firearm. He answered: "Not at that moment." When he was asked if the woman who found the gun was carrying it in a safe manner, he said: "Yes."

Those were the facts.

(I have all the transcripts from the court hearings I am writing about. The court commissioner's hearing was recorded. I have listened to that recording many times to make sure I heard it all correctly. I also have all of the witnesses written reports.)

Apparently, the court commissioner never read the witness reports. I don't know from where the statement he made had originated.

The statement the court commissioner made, as recorded in the transcript and which I can only think was his probable cause for a crime, was that "someone could have come upon the weapon."

"Someone could have"? Oh yes! "Someone could have" seems to be what established probable cause for the court commissioner to make the legal decision that there was enough probable cause to not dismiss the case but to pass it on to a judge.

Try to imagine the number of people who could be charged with a crime if "someone could have" is probable cause:

- *The preschool teacher left the sharp scissors on her desk before school started while she went to the bathroom and "someone could have."*
- *He left the electric saw plugged in while he went inside for lunch and "someone could have."*
- *The volunteer in the church kitchen left the sharp knife unattended for an hour and "someone could have."*

If probable cause to charge someone with the crime of endangering safety is that "someone could have" or "something could have happened" but didn't, we would need to have more prosecutors, more court commissioners, more judges, more staff, more jails, and higher taxes.

How many of us have done something accidentally, or even on purpose, in which "something could have happened" or "someone could have been hurt" but nothing did happen? Given the right circumstances and a prosecutor motivated in an area other than the law, a criminal charge could be the result and even a conviction. I read countless examples of this really occurring.

What a door this opens for prosecutors who want to rack up more prosecutions!

This is not just about a firearm. It could have, and has, been about other "someone could haves" or "something could haves." It could certainly include sharp knives left on a countertop in a school or church kitchen, cars left running in parking lots while the owner was not in the car (and I know of four people in the same family who have done that with those push-button start cars).

It would eventually, unfortunately, lead to including dangerous tools in garages with the garage door left open, toxic cleaning materials under a kitchen sink at home and in public places such as schools and churches. These are all incidences where "someone could have" or "something could have." Believe that nothing so obviously nonsensical, illogical, and vague could ever pass the test of being legal? Stay tuned.

A case very much like this happened in late 2018 in Ozaukee County, Wisconsin. A young woman was charged, not with a misdemeanor, but with a felony—a felony! She was taking a plastic wading pool to her sister's house. She didn't think it would fit in her van, so she put it on the roof, and then had her son ride up there to hold the pool in place during a short drive to her sister's house.

She told police her dad let her do things like that when she was young. She had her son strapped down on top of the pool on the vehicle's roof. The ride lasted twenty to thirty seconds before she moved her son back inside, and shoved the pool in, too. The person who called the police saw her drive that twenty to thirty seconds and then take her son down.[2]

Yes, initial bad judgement which she corrected quickly. Nothing happened to her son.

What law did the DA of Ozaukee County use to charge this young woman with a felony?

Wisconsin State Statute 941.30

Recklessly endangering safety

(1) FIRST-DEGREE RECKLESSLY ENDANGERING SAFETY. Whoever recklessly endangers another's safety under circumstances which show utter disregard for human life is guilty of a Class F felony.

(2) SECOND-DEGREE RECKLESSLY ENDANGERING SAFETY. Whoever recklessly endangers another's safety is guilty of a Class G felony.

Did this young woman recklessly endanger the safety of her son? Is she a criminal? A felon? This is a young single woman with children. A felony will be on her record for the rest of her life. Any job she applies for, she will have to confess that she is a felon. She was guilty of momentary bad judgment, sure, but there indeed wasn't any criminal intent, and nothing happened to anyone. She corrected the situation within seconds. She not only didn't have criminal intent; she didn't commit a criminal action.

This charge can only be based on "something could have" happened. That's all the DA of Ozaukee County needed to charge this young woman with a felony, i.e., "something could have happened." He charged this young woman with second degree recklessly endangering safety.

Why would he do that? Maybe that it is just what this DA of a county with very little crime thought he needed to do to justify his job? I don't know. But to ruin a young woman's life for momentary bad judgment, which she corrected with no one getting harmed, is an overreach to the max!

She is now officially a felon, as she was convicted in April 2018 when she was charged with a Class G felony. She could not afford to hire an attorney. She had a public defender who didn't use the Constitution and the law to free her client from this unfair tragedy. Just like in my case, this charge should have been dismissed as no probable cause.

Wisconsin State Statute 939.50

Classification of felonies

For a Class G felony there is a fine not to exceed $25,000 or imprisonment not to exceed 10 years, or both.

This felony conviction will have collateral damage to this twenty-six-year-old woman with children for the rest of her life. "Something could have happened" and an over-charging prosecutor stole the rest of this young woman's life—now and in her future. The unchecked power of a prosecutor who is not held accountable has ruined many lives.

By the way,I never felt any resentment for the person who called the police from the church when my firearm was found. The church allowed concealed carry but there was never a protocol regarding what to do if a firearm was found unattended anywhere in the church.

In fact, not only were there not any feelings of resentment or anger, now, I am thankful. The opportunity this gave me to research and then report on the frightful number of people who have been harmed by a prosecutor with a purpose other than the law is a door that would never have been opened for me any other way.

Some people who have known me for a long time said something to the effect that they were sorry that this happened to me. But if it had to happen to somebody, they were glad it was me because, as many people said to me, "You will fight back." I didn't possess a "fighting back mindset" at that time, but I sure did get one later. Discovering that my prosecutor experience was far from rare but had happened to countless others, I had to fight back. This wasn't just about me.

All of Us are Affected by "No Probable Cause" Cases

The only fact that the court commissioner needed to make a legal decision about my case was to follow the law written by the Legislative Branch and plainly recorded in the Wisconsin State statute. Specifically, Wisconsin State Statute 948.55, as quoted previously. Not one other thing made a legal difference.

A judicial inference that "someone could have" is not probable cause to charge anyone with a crime. In my non-attorney mind, if the law as written had merely been followed, no charges should have ever been made.

Taxpayer money, the crowded court calendar, all the negative effects for everyone could have been avoided had the Wisconsin State statute been followed. Instead, the prosecutor obviously searched the statutes to find a law that could be twisted in an apparent attempt to fit her agenda instead of ministering true justice based on fact.

As I started to realize how much time and money it took for my case when there was never a legal reason to issue one criminal charge—let alone two—I could not help but wonder if the crowded court calendar and taxpayer money is too often spent to satisfy a prosecutor's own purposes and not the law's. An inappropriate use of the court system not only costs the wrongfully accused—it costs all of us.

At every step—from the police, to the prosecutor, to the district attorney, to the court commissioner—the law as written was ignored entirely. The Constitution was ignored. The rule of law was ignored.

The Rule of Law

The rule of law requires the government to exercise its power in accordance with well-established and clearly written rules, regulations, and legal principles.

Under the rule of law, no person may be prosecuted for an act that is not punishable by law. When the government seeks to punish someone for an offense that was not deemed criminal at the time it was committed, the rule of law is violated because the government exceeds its legal authority to punish. The rule of law requires that government impose liability only insofar as the law will allow.[3]

Not one government official followed the rule of law—not one! And I'm the alleged criminal? I, thank God, I didn't harm anyone with my much regretted, although unintentional, act. How many people have been harmed by the reckless, intentional ignoring of the established safeguards for citizens—the Constitution, the separation of powers, and the rule of law by our government officials?

Even though my attorney offered a totally legal defense of no probable cause and what certainly appears to be no legitimate probable cause given by the court commissioner, my case was passed on to a judge. Defense Attorney Grieve told me it would. I expected that.

It was only after the research and connecting with others who have had similar experiences with the criminal courts, that I woke up to what happened to me. I slowly began to realize that my experience spoke to how our justice system has strayed far from what the founders of our country, who wrote the Constitution and the Bill of Rights, ever intended.

A court date with Judge Lloyd Carter was set for June 9, 2014. I opted not to appear by signing an Authorization to Appear form, which was my choice to do. Of course, my attorney did appear. He reported to me that Judge Carter "took the matter under advisement" and set another court date for June 19, 2014.

Attorney Grieve told me that this was a good sign. He also informed me that the prosecutor who charged me did not appear in court but sent an underling.

On June 19, 2014, Case Dismissed

Judge Carter dismissed the charge of endangering safety, stating that this was like someone leaving their car running with the key in, but nothing happened.

Whew!

This is when I started to realize that if had I been charged with a crime, it could open the door for many other "someone could have" or "something could have happened" criminal charges in many incidents for many people.

Interestingly, my attorney, Tom Grieve, reported that the

prosecutor had indicated that she believed she had not gotten a conviction because she had not named a person directly endangered. Attorney Grieve had already told her that in his motion to dismiss.: "To endanger the safety of another means that someone must have been directly endangered by the actions of the defendant…"

Now, she could have issued the same charge against me but named who was directly endangered. Of course, she couldn't do that because no one was directly endangered.

Well, that was just a mere setback for the prosecutor.

Even though the first criminal charge was dismissed by Judge Carter as not having any facts to support a probable cause for a crime… Even though a written law perfectly defined why I had not committed a crime… Evidently, ignoring all the negative effects on everyone else and, seemingly, with her mind set firmly on winning… in less than one month, the prosecutor once again issued criminal charges for the same unintentional act.

The power of prosecutors is also exploding. Even when law enforcement is at its best, prosecution must be selective; not enough resources exist to pursue everyone… Some targets are chosen for tactical reasons, to impress other potential targets. Some targeting is… political ambition.

If prosecutors were to bear a risk similar to medical malpractice for bringing unjustified cases to court, there might be a more efficient use of prosecutorial resources…and prosecutors might focus their attention on crimes for which they had real evidence

Paul Craig Roberts and Lawrence M. Stratton, *The Tyranny of Good Intentions: How Prosecutors and Law Enforcement are Trampling the Constitution in the Name of Justice*

Notes Chapter 4

1   The title of a 1963 movie which became a (bad 🙂) pick-up
     line and ultimately a cliché
2   Bruce Vielmetti, "Mom who drove with 9-year-old son
     on roof of her van pleads guilty to felony," *Journal Sentinel*,
     March 15, 2018, https://www.jsonline.com/story/news/
     crime/2018/03/15/mom-who-drove-9-year-old-son-roof-
     her-van-pleads-guilty-felony/428396002/
3   "Rule of law," The Legal Dictionary, https://legal-dictionary.
     thefreedictionary.com/rule+of+law

Chapter 5

The "Play it Again" Prosecutor

September 14, 2014

The prosecutor threatened, via my attorney, to charge me with criminal disorderly conduct (Wisconsin State Statute 947.01) unless I gave up my concealed carry rights for a specific amount of time, pay a fine, forfeit my firearm, and admit to committing a crime when I didn't.

The criminal court system calls that a plea bargain. Plea bargaining is discussed in Chapter 12. And how the prosecutor may have come up with the 2nd charge is presented in Chapter 11.

Personally, I think that the prosecutor was exceedingly ticked off because, based on my emotional condition in the "pre-charge" interview, she figured that I would "go down" without a fight easily and fast. I didn't.

For the second time, the prosecutor wanted me to incriminate myself. She wanted me to admit to committing a crime when the law written by the Legislative Branch of government stated that a crime was never committed. My right to not incriminate myself doesn't count in a plea bargain.

The Fifth Amendment of our Constitution states that "no person shall be compelled in any criminal case to be a witness against himself." Unfortunately, it appears that the Department of Justice gets to decide what that means. The Fifth Amendment doesn't count if you are "compelled to be a witness against yourself" because of a plea bargain.

September 23, 2014

After hearing what the prosecutor would do to me if I didn't lie and say that I committed a crime, my husband asked me to please "give her something," as he was worried about my health. My husband had a good reason for concern. I was visibly an emotional wreck. I was sleeping very little and would start crying often. This is just not like me. I have survived breast cancer (chemo, radiation), a life-threatening staph infection after a hip replacement, and just months before being criminally charged along with the resultant media "reporting," a heart attack. I was never this visibly upset with any of that as I had been with this ordeal. I was undoubtedly miserable physically with those illnesses, but my spirits were generally high.

Based on my husband's concern, via my attorney, I offered my firearm as well as to take a safety course (I had already taken several). I did not want to do this, as I felt that I was being intimidated and threatened to admit to a crime when I didn't commit one and, even more distressing, to have a criminal record. However, with all my husband and I had gone through with my health, I agreed.

Plea bargain? It was then that I began to question how a government employee could have that much power. That's why it only took days for me to regret that decision to relinquish my firearm and take a firearms safety course. I felt as if I was being blackmailed.

I was not going to be coerced into lying. Lying wasn't the only reason I changed my mind. By then, I had read enough to know that this could be a precedent. That might mean that other people could be charged with an unintentional act where no one was hurt. This was a "toe in the door" for more laws as well as a prosecutor essentially making law. I also saw it as another attack on Second Amendment rights.

I called my attorney and asked him if he had heard from the prosecutor—he told me no, he hadn't. I asked him to rescind the offer of offering my firearm and taking a safety course. I was not going to lie and incriminate myself when the Wisconsin State statutes clearly stated that no crime had been committed.

I knew that meant that the prosecutor would, once again, carry out her threat to charge me with a crime. Once again, I would be exposed to the media and portrayed as a criminal. Once again, we would be paying attorney fees to defend me.

Apparently, Attorney Grieve didn't inform her of my decision to rescind the offer. He may have wanted to know what she would do with a fair offer. After all, we knew that the DA had at least one case like mine and had the person take a safety course. I was offering that and giving up my personal property.

I was ultimately pleased that she didn't know that I had rescinded my offer. So, she still believed my offer stood.

November 25, 2014

Two months (speedy trial?) later, my attorney received this email:

> Attorney Grieve,
>
> I apologize for the delay in responding to you regarding Ms. Hitchler's case, but the facts continue to trouble me. I am unwilling to accept your offer.

(She then stated her most recent punishment for me if I refused her offer: She demanded (1) my personal property—my firearm—and my Second Amendment rights to be forfeited for a specified period of time, (2) a fine—more than what she wanted for the first charge—and (3) admitting to a crime I did not commit.)

> Please let me know at your earliest convenience if this is acceptable to you and your client. If it is not, I intend to issue the DC (disorderly conduct) criminal charge.

Thank you,

________, Assistant District Attorney, Waukesha County

First, remember what constitutes probable cause to charge someone with a crime: facts. Does the prosecutor's statement in her email — "the facts continue to trouble me" —constitute probable cause for a criminal charge? The facts troubled *her*. What facts?

The facts, according to the Wisconsin State statutes, states that there wasn't a crime.

A prosecutor is a tax-paid employee of the government. His or her priority is not to serve their own interests. The prosecutor's first and foremost responsibility is to serve the best interest of the citizens and not of themselves. They are charged to interpret and follow the laws written by the Legislative Branch of government.

What the prosecutor wants or what "troubles" that prosecutor isn't supposed to matter, but it often does!

What did my attorney say about all of this? What could he say? Prosecutors can do anything they want. They can charge anyone, anytime, with anything. The only option anyone can do is to represent themselves or hire an attorney. No one, not even a defense attorney, can stop a prosecutor from issuing a criminal charge even if the attorney knows full well there is no probable cause. All anyone can do is go to court and present their case.

Before Attorney Grieve informed the prosecutor that I was refusing her offer, he had to tell me what could happen if I were charged with disorderly conduct: I could be fined $10,000 and even go to jail. It was his duty to make sure I knew what the maximum punishment could be if we didn't prevail this time.

Jail and $10,000 for not committing a crime? I can only say that I have read enough true stories to know people who never committed a crime according to the law but, despite that, ended up in jail.

When Attorney Grieve told the prosecutor of my refusal, she

attempted to persuade me, via my attorney, to change my mind. She told Attorney Grieve, "Wouldn't it be great for the media to show up and your client wouldn't be there?"

Oh yes—good grief—that would make up for all the unnecessary stress, exposure, and demonization by the media, the expense, and the pain and all that has happened to me thanks to the prosecutor. The prosecutor, who issued a "no probable cause" criminal charge once and now was blackmailing me with even more dire consequences than the first time. Attorney Grieve told the prosecutor that he would inform his client, me, but doubted that his client would change her mind.

He was right—I didn't change my mind.

Consequently, and with the full permission of the DA, the prosecutor issued criminal charges on November 27, 2014. She charged me with criminal disorderly conduct.

Wisconsin State Statute 947.01

Disorderly conduct

(1) Whoever, in a public or private place, engages in violent, abusive, indecent, profane, boisterous, unreasonably loud or otherwise Disorderly Conduct under circumstances in which the conduct tends to cause or provoke a disturbance is guilty of a Class B misdemeanor.

Remember the facts of this case: firearm there for less than five minutes, no children around (in fact, very few people in the vicinity), and only two adults touched the firearm. There was no violent, abusive, indecent, profane, boisterous, or unreasonably loud behavior.

How could I have engaged in any such thing? I wasn't there. There was not a disturbance. How could someone who wasn't there provoke something that never happened?

(2) Unless other facts and circumstances that indicate a criminal or malicious intent on the part of the person apply, a person is not in violation of, and may not be charged with a violation of, this section for loading a firearm, or for carrying or going armed with a firearm or a knife, without regard to whether the firearm is loaded or the firearm or the knife is concealed or openly carried.

My act was unintentional. There was no malicious intent. Despite this, it is evident that a prosecutor's arbitrary reason for issuing a criminal charge was okay with the Waukesha County Criminal Court System. It seems just as apparent that concern for the law as written, the rule of law, mens rea (a criminal intent), constitutional rights, damage to an innocent person and family, and the taxpayers are of no concern.

That despite what is on the official website:

> *"Welcome to the Waukesha County Circuit Courts website… Waukesha County court system are committed to providing a fair and efficient system of justice that is worthy of the trust and confidence of the public."* [1]

I would guess that something like that is on every justice department website.

Unless one had experienced what I did, what so many others have, that statement would probably be believed.

On the Same Day That Charge Was Made Official

Nik Clark, president of Wisconsin Carry, and his organization's attorneys released this public condemnation:

Wisconsin Carry Condemns Waukesha County DA's Office Action…

Waukesha County ADA ______ filed charges of negligent handling of a weapon: Wis. Stat. 941.20(1)(a) against Susan. At the time, Wisconsin Carry representatives, interviewed by local media, suggested this charge did not in any way seem appropriate for the situation.

A Waukesha County judge agreed, and the case was thrown out of court on June 19th. All charges dismissed.

In what can only be described as a misguided prosecutorial over-reach, Assistant District Attorney _______ was undeterred. After having the initial bogus charge tossed out of court, over the course of the summer, ADA _______ threatened Susan with an even more bogus charge of "disorderly conduct" unless Susan willingly agreed to give up her concealed carry license for LIFE and forfeit her expensive gun.

...Wisconsin has a law that specifically addresses leaving or storing a gun where a child could gain access to it. WI's Stat. 948.55.

Susan refused to cede her Constitutional right to self-defense for the rest of her life, nor her private property, to the demands of ADA _______. As threatened, ADA _____ filed charges of "disorderly conduct" against Susan this past Tuesday (November 24th).

Wisconsin Carry condemns the actions of Waukesha County Assistant District Attorney _______. While Susan's mistake was careless and highly embarrassing, no crime occurred.

When passing 948.55, the Wisconsin legislature CLEARLY considered what should and should not be a crime when it comes to leaving a gun where a child can gain access to it. They clearly intended that leaving a gun within easy access of a child would not be a crime unless a child obtained, discharged, and injured someone with the gun.

Wisconsin Carry believes prosecutors should use discretion deciding how to enforce the laws of the state of Wisconsin. Under NO circumstances should prosecutors attempt to legislate from the DA's office prosecuting behaviors that the legislature has decided should not be crimes.

In addition to being a waste of taxpayer resources by the Waukesha County DA's office, citizens of Waukesha County should be concerned what other non-crimes law-abiding citizens may be persecuted for via prosecution in the future.

If you would like to ask the Waukesha County DA to stop persecuting gun owners and leave the creation of law to the legislature contact the office of the District Attorney

Carry On,

Nik Clark

Chairman/President—Wisconsin Carry, Inc.[2]

According to my attorney, the DA's office was furious with this public condemnation of their actions. Could it be that they don't like the public to know what goes on behind closed doors?

Nik Clark, who has been a tremendous support to me, told me that there were hundreds of emails, calls, and letters that were sent to the Waukesha County DA supporting the condemnation and all the objections to the prosecutor's actions and the fact that the DA's office was allowing her to carry out her criminal charges against me. Perhaps that was the motivation for the prosecutor to change her plea bargain offer.

On **December 7, 2014**, the prosecutor made me a "kinder, gentler" plea bargain offer (less of a fine and less time without my

Second Amendment rights). In other words, a "kinder, gentler" blackmail option.

My attorney told the prosecutor that he would inform me of her offer but doubted that I would accept it. He told me that he also said to her: "Susan is a principled person."

He was right, I refused. So off we went to court again.

Lord Acton writes to Bishop Creighton that the same moral standards should be applied to all men, political and religious leaders included, especially since *"Power tends to corrupt and absolute power corrupts absolutely"* (1887)

Notes Chapter 5

1   Waukesha Circuit Courts, https://www.waukeshacounty.gov/circuitcourts/

2   Nik Clark, "Wisconsin Carry Condemns Waukesha County DA's Office Action," November 27, 2014, http://www.wisconsincarry.org/news/wisconsin-carry-condemns-waukesha-county-das-office-action.aspx

The first time I entered prosecutor misconduct into a search engine, this was the initial article that I found. What I had been thinking was confirmed - something was wrong with what was done to me by an employee of our government.

Overly aggressive prosecutors again BY PENNY HERSCHER (2011)

"Being charged with a crime ruins your life. No question, whether you are innocent or guilty your life and career are put on hold and all focus goes to defending yourself. And, in our society, whether right or not, people are assumed guilty until proven innocent...

Which is why it is so wrong that prosecutors can get away with pursuing someone for a crime when there is simply not enough evidence to charge him and ruin his life - and have no consequence themselves

Given how devastating being prosecuted is why is there not more public outrage when prosecutors step on ordinary Americans rights to advance their political agendas?

Chapter 6

Encore, The Court Commissioner

December 8, 2014 Preliminary Hearing

Back to the same court commissioner for Round #2.

The mainstream media was there again. But this time with a cameraman only. No reporter. (Is it possible that I was no longer the most dangerous granny in Waukesha County?) I asked the cameraman what awful criminal would he be filming for the day's news; was it that terrible grandmother again? He said "No," not her. Of course, it was. Amazing.

I had an appointment with my orthopedic surgeon that afternoon. I had been having some trouble with my hip replacement and was using a cane. The "always waiting for a moment to misrepresent the politically incorrect" mainstream media camera guy took a picture when I was looking down at my cane. I suspect that it would look like the judge had been so stern with me for the criminal activities that I couldn't hold up my head.

That media-created fantasy was, once again, not true.

In fact, I was looking forward to how the court commissioner would find any kind of probable cause for criminal disorderly conduct to pass this latest charge of a criminal action on to a judge. By then, I had done enough research to underline my initial supposition that "someone could have" was not probable cause for a crime.

The prosecutor's stated email reason for issuing another criminal charge—i.e., the facts troubled her—is also obviously not probable cause of a crime. Read the law and compare with the facts. Did I engage in violent, abusive, indecent, profane, boisterous, unreasonably loud or otherwise disorderly conduct that tended to cause or provoke a disturbance? No. Was this an intentional malicious act? No.

That being the case, our thirteen-year-old grandson had reached the conclusion of "no probable cause" for a crime long before the legal professionals did. He didn't need a law degree to reach that conclusion. He didn't need to pass the Bar. He had something far better and much less expensive: common sense.

Trickle-Down Misconduct

It's more like flooding down.

From my research, it appears that this kind of behavior started at the federal level. Because there were no consequences—no punishment when prosecutors violated the Constitution, rule of law, ethical behavior, applying the law as written, and hiding exculpatory evidence that would clear a defendant of a crime—the realization that anything goes was evident. Because convictions were rewarded despite violations of the protections for the safety of citizens, more and more prosecutors engaged in unethical and illegal behavior.

Sadly, not only is it ignored—and, therefore, allowed—but that behavior is frequently rewarded.

"Is it any wonder the misconduct doesn't stop? The incentive isn't there. After all, a high-profile prosecution can turn a prosecutor into a local celebrity… launch a political career. Even something as serious as "reckless professional misconduct" merits little more than short suspension. Sometimes, however, misconduct merits a promotion."

Jay Sekulow, *Undemocratic: How Unelected, Unaccountable Bureaucrats are Stealing Your Liberty and Freedom*

The prosecutor was promoted from assistant district attorney to deputy district attorney on February 8, 2015. That promotion puts her in a managerial type position. She can supervise, mentor, and instruct other prosecutors. Will her supervision, mentoring, and instructing of other prosecutors include observing the rights, ethics, laws, and the separation of powers that exist to protect people?

I don't know how it could.

What Will the Court Commissioner Do?

I sat in anticipation of what the court commissioner could possibly find as probable cause to pass the charge of criminal disorderly conduct on to a judge.

So, what did the court commissioner do? Nothing.

My attorney said, "Judge."

The prosecutor said, "Judge."

And that was that. A court date with a judge was set for March 3, 2015. Attorney Grieve never told me he was going to excuse the court commissioner from having to decide. I didn't even know that was possible.

At first, I was a bit angry. But, as I thought about it, I knew why he didn't tell me. By then, since I had come back into "myself" after being a sleepless, depressed, stressed out, panicky mess, he knew that I would probably ask him to let the court commissioner figure it out or dismiss the case.

Now, I am so pleased that Attorney Grieve did what he did. I was delighted way before to writing a book even entered my mind[1]. Charging me for the second time allowed me to underscore the conclusions I was reaching about the exploding and unchecked power of a prosecutor.

Often what we see as "How could you allow this to happen, Lord?" turns out to be a blessing.

Back to Court We Go…But First

This time I decided to be in court. The last time I signed a statement (Authorization to Appear) that said I didn't need to be in court, so I didn't go. In retrospect, I wish I would have gone that first time too. I can see the benefit to the entire system if the accused doesn't appear in court. The accused might learn too much. I did.

It was around this time that I got my tongue-in-cheek, stress-relieving, sanity-saving sense of humor back. That humor has been useful in my personal and professional life. When I was seriously ill, it was that humor that helped me keep perspective and faith.

There were only two times when I could not use my humor to relieve my stress and to give me perspective. The first was during that staph infection. One of the antibiotics affected me emotionally. You have probably heard warnings with certain medications. If the mentioned side effects occur, your doctor must be contacted immediately. One of those side effects are thoughts of suicide.

There are other emotional and mental symptoms that medications can produce that echo a clinical depression. Those can include acute anxiety, panic attacks, crying far more often than usual, disturbing dreams, and so on. I had all of those from one of the antibiotics I was either taking by mouth or receiving through a pic line that had been inserted in my arm.

For three months I experienced these symptoms, which were far worse than the physical pain and discomfort. The doctors wouldn't take me off that medication because it was being used to save my life. Anti-depressants didn't help. Within twenty-four hours of quitting that antibiotic, I was fine.

The second time that I could not use my humor to "lighten the load," so to speak, was when I was charged as a criminal and portrayed as one in the mainstream media. The first court appearance, the harassment and pictures by the media, the hurtful comments by some people, the mug shot, fingerprinting, and humiliation of being treated like a criminal was devastating.

Thankfully, my ability to use humor did come back after that second criminal charge. I say *thankfully* because adding a little humor helped me immensely when writing these next two chapters.

Humor Helps—Really!

I learned a long time ago in my professional speaking career, when I began to specialize in difficult and challenging audiences, that you can say stronger things with a sense of humor than you can without. (Of course, actually having a sense of humor is essential!)

I honestly don't know how to accurately present a real-life feeling for the lack of common sense, the disrespect for the law, the total uncaring and lack of concern for the innocent person, and the unbelievable excuse for the logic of two prosecutors without being able to take it a bit more lightly—a little "comic relief." The ridiculousness of what passes for due process, probable cause, and logic in the American justice system is terrifying. It is hard to believe that any of this could be true. Not only true of the prosecutors in my "obscure" case, but true in massive amounts of cases by a vast number of prosecutors.

The night before we were due in court, the prosecution sent a twenty-page probable cause for criminal disorderly conduct to my attorney. These twenty pages ostensibly gave factual evidence (probable cause) of how I intentionally caused a disturbance, which rose to the level of being a crime necessitating criminal punishment.

There will be some tongue-in cheek moments. That type of humor illustrates truth in a playful, funny way. It takes what is really being done or said to the point of ridiculousness to reveal the lack of logic and common sense.

Notes Chapter 6

[1]*"When you realize that God will put ideas in your mind, that's when the adventure begins".*

Pete Briscoe

"The misdemeanor system punishes people too heavily and in too many ways for minor, common, and often harmless conduct"

Alexandra Natapoff *Punishment Without Crime: How are massive misdemeanor system traps the innocent and makes America more unequal*

We have a bloated misdemeanor system that is costing us our freedom and our money. Many of the books in my bibliography touched on this. In Jay Sekulow's book *"Undemocratic"* He has an entire Chapter titled: *"Making it Up as They Go Along".* We have an oppressive, overbearing, and arbitrary system in America and it is getting more so everyday

Chapter 7

Turning Legal Logic into an Oxymoron

Probable cause to charge someone with a crime means that there is "sufficient reason based upon known facts to believe a crime has been committed."[1]

Of course, as we already know, there is a specific law that relates exactly to my case. Taking the facts of what happened and applying those known facts to Wisconsin State Statute 948.55, clearly, no crime was committed; there was no legislative probable cause for a criminal charge.

The responsibility of the Judicial Branch of government is to take the laws written by the Legislative Branch and interpret and apply them. There is no other way to interpret Wisconsin State Statute 948.55 but to reach the conclusion that a crime was not committed.

In several of the articles and books I read, the use of "creative" and far-fetched reasons to establish probable cause by a prosecutor and obtain a conviction was given. I could not imagine how a prosecutor could create an improbable probable cause, much less have a court of law even take the time with a crowded calendar, waste the taxpayer's money, and put a citizen through the ordeal of criminal court with an utterly improbable probable cause.

I no longer need to imagine how.

My attorney emailed me the twenty-page brief, which the prosecutor submitted late in the day before our court date. This brief was supposedly the "proof" that the prosecutor's charge of criminal disorderly conduct had the facts that would establish probable cause. (Actually, the twenty-page brief was written by the junior prosecutor with, I would assume, the prosecutor's oversight and approval.)

It took me countless readings of that brief to untangle and make sense out of what was being asserted as facts for issuing a criminal charge.

A prosecutor must possess enough facts that would lead a reasonable person to believe that a criminal charge is warranted. Here, I will present the "facts" that were ascertained by the prosecutors to establish probable cause for a criminal charge as clearly as I possibly can.

Criminal Disorderly Conduct Must Include Two Elements

Two elements are required for a charge of disorderly conduct: (1) mens rea: intent—a guilty mind, criminal intent; and (2) the causing of a disturbance.[2]

This is what Attorney Grieve wrote in the motion to dismiss:

> "Specifically, the complaint fails to set forth essential facts from which it could be inferred that the defendant committed a crime and fails to state the essential facts constituting the offense charged as required by law."

The State needed to supply the facts that both the intention to commit a crime as well as the causing of a disturbance are present. In other words, the prosecutor had to establish that I intentionally forgot my firearm and in intentionally forgetting my firearm, I knew that I was committing the crime of criminal disorderly conduct. (First, consider how someone can intentionally forget? Sound like an oxymoron right from the start.)

Here is what was written in the brief to factually prove that I forgot my firearm on purpose with criminal intent:

"...she was given proper notice that her conduct was prohibited by law and someone with average intelligence would know such conduct is prohibited."

The prosecutors were stating, as a fact, that I knew that forgetting my firearm in a bathroom was prohibited by law. Therefore, I had criminal intent because I forgot my gun on purpose, fully knowing that I was committing a crime.

What?

How did these two prosecutors "prove" as a known fact that I had forgotten my firearm intentionally? How did they "prove" as a known fact that I knew that I had committed the crime of criminal disorderly conduct?

Just have faith, dear readers, our "heroines of justice" have it all figured out. And, if I dare say—It's a hoot.

The Prosecutor's Precedent Case

Next, in the twenty-page brief, the prosecutors cited a case (*City of Oak Creek v. King*) which they were contending was a precedent for their criminal charge of criminal disorderly conduct against me. They were using this case to prove the requirement of intent (mens rea).

In *City of Oak Creek v. King,* a news reporter jumped over a fence intentionally and took pictures of a plane crash after being asked to leave a restricted area by police. This person intentionally ignored the instruction of the police officer. He was given proper notice that his behavior was prohibited by the law via an officer of the law.

The reporter avoided the police and did what they asked him not to do. The reporter was chased by the police, who again asked him to leave the area. The reporter said he would not leave until he was arrested. That reporter's actions were obviously intentional. A police officer—the law—gave this reporter proper notice that his behavior was prohibited—several times.

From that case, which the two prosecutors cited as precedent for my case, they wrote that I "was given proper notice that her conduct was prohibited by law…" They are contending that because the reporter in that case, who was given verbal instructions by an officer of the law—i.e., given proper notice that his conduct was prohibited by law—was precedent for my case.

> Precedent is a legal principle, created by a court decision, which provides an example or authority for judges deciding similar issues later. Generally, decisions of higher courts (within a particular system of courts) are mandatory precedents on lower courts within that system. That means the principle announced by a higher court must be followed in later cases.[3]
>
> A prior reported opinion of an appeals court which establishes the legal rule (authority) in the future on the same legal question decided in the prior judgment.[4]

Of course, the case that our prosecutors used as precedent for my case did not come from a higher court. However, the real issue here is: How do the actions of the reporter in the alleged precedent case have any similarities to my case in any way? The reporter intentionally refused to follow a direct order from an officer of the law. He led the police on a chase and refused to obey their orders unless they arrested him. In what way did these two prosecutors think that this was any kind of legal precedent for a criminal charge in my case?

Perhaps I am being too harsh here. But, how could anyone with any degree of common sense, with the ability to think with even the most straightforward logic, ever conclude that someone would know that forgetting a firearm in a public place was the crime of disorderly conduct?

> *"Thus, more and more innocent conduct gets swept into the*
> *category of crime—not by legislatures, and only secondarily*
> *by judges and juries, but primarily by these dangerous*
> *and altogether too common prosecutorial practices."*

Harvey A. Silverglate, *Three Felonies a Day*

Bottom line: In the opinion of these two prosecutors, they had legally proven intent based on what they had decided with their legally trained and experienced minds was a precedent case because it was "similar" to mine.

The Need to Prove the Causing of a Disturbance

The need to prove that my actions caused a disturbance is the second element that needs to be present to prove—to have probable cause—for the criminal charge of disorderly conduct. The prosecutors obviously believed that they "proved" their assertion that I had, not only, intentionally forgotten my firearm, but that I also knew that I was committing a crime because:

> "...the Defendant was upset when discussing with police how she left her gun at the church and even stated that she could not believe she had done this. It was clear that the Defendant knew her conduct was unreasonable, indecent, and dangerous, because no one would feel upset or be in disbelief had it not been so offensive and contrary to the norms of the community."

In Chapter 1, I wrote what I said to the police officer who called me. Through tears, I told the officer that I could not believe I had done that, i.e., forgot to put my gun back in place. I meant I was surprised, disappointed, and upset with myself because I had always been a careful and vigilant firearm owner.

In Chapter 1, I noted that the prosecutor would take that sentence and twist it into something that would suit her need. She did.

The junior prosecutor and the prosecutor took one sentence given to a police officer, and spun, twisted, and distorted that one sentence into meaning that not only did I intentionally forget my firearm but that I knew my "conduct was unreasonable, indecent, and dangerous."

In addition to that, they took one sentence and used it to seemingly "prove" that the whole community was upset.

> "…because no one would feel upset or be in disbelief had it not been so offensive and contrary to the norms of the community."

My jaw still drops when I read that.

These prosecutors in the criminal justice system were stating it as a *fact* in a *legal document* contending that their prosecutorial mind-reading was evidence of probable cause for a criminal charge. In other words, they are stating as a fact, that the moment I forgot my firearm I knew that my "conduct was unreasonable, indecent, and dangerous, because no one would feel upset or be in disbelief had it not been so offensive and contrary to the norms of the community."

Your Honor, I object! (As long as we aren't dealing in factual reality anymore, I think I will make myself an attorney!)

Still, our "legal eagles" had the problem of connecting the case (*City of Oak Creek v. King*) they used as precedent in prosecuting my case. Although they just stated that I knew I had upset an entire community, they apparently presumed that they had better prove that the entire community was, indeed, upset and offended.

In *King*, the defendant was found guilty not because, as the

Wisconsin State Statute 947.01 defines disorderly conduct as "violent, abusive, indecent, profane, boisterous, unreasonably loud or otherwise disorderly conduct under circumstances in which the conduct tends to cause or provoke a disturbance" but because, according to the *King* case, "the conduct was disturbing in the eyes of the reasonable person and offends the sense of decency in the community."[5]

Of course, now the junior prosecutor, with the oversight of the prosecutor, had to prove that the entire community was disturbed by a firearm left in a bathroom for under five minutes with no children present and very few adults. Here is what they used as proof this time:

> "...average persons of ordinary intelligence would consider the Defendant's conduct disturbing as demonstrated by the multiple news stories regarding the incident. The fact that there were multiple news stories about the Defendant's conduct demonstrates that our community was outraged by her conduct."

(Get ready for some necessary humor—at least it was necessary for me at this point!) I started to call this Unicorn Logic. It goes something like this:

> **Prosecutor:** "Your Honor, the fact that there are pictures of unicorns proves that they are real."

> **Defense Attorney:** "Excuse me, Your Honor, but those are caricatures. They aren't pictures of real, live unicorns."

> **Prosecutor:** "The average persons of ordinary intelligence would consider that caricatures of unicorns appearing in printed media such as books and cartoons and the fact that they also appear in movies and on TV would demonstrate that unicorns are real."

Defense Attorney: "Your Honor, may I request a brief recess? I need to go outside to scream and punch the side of the building a few times."

Judge: "Me too! Would ten minutes be okay?"

Defense Attorney: "Twenty minutes may be necessary if it pleases Your Honor."

Judge: "I concur, twenty minutes it is."

Tongue-in-cheek humor serves the purpose of taking something to its most ridiculous level in order to expose the truth. There is an old saying: "You cannot enlighten the unconscious."

What is alarming is that Unicorn Logic would make sense not only to some prosecutors, but some judges. In some of the many cases that I read, it did. If the prosecutors' Unicorn Logic—i.e., "multiple" news stories—were the legal guidelines for determining the charge of criminal disorderly conduct, there would be scores of people who could be charged with criminal disorderly conduct.

Ironically, the DA could have been charged with criminal disorderly conduct based on the prosecutor's probable cause argument written by the junior prosecutor. Multiple news stories and editorials from outraged citizens cited the DA's refusal to charge a man who left a bar, fell asleep at the wheel, and killed a man riding a bicycle. The DA said he couldn't think of anything with which to charge him. (He should have asked the prosecutor—recklessly endangering safety [Statute 941.30] and criminal disorderly conduct [Statute 947.01], right?)

I can think of other people who could be charged with criminal disorderly conduct because of the multiple news stories about them. Political figures? Sports figures? Hollywood? That is not an exhaustive list, I am quite sure. Did the community's outrage cause the media to publish these news stories in any cases like the above, including mine?

By the way, this twenty-page report actually included the news stories.

Those Were The "Facts" That Established Probable Cause?

In my opinion, this and the rest of that long brief contained some of the most convoluted, ill-conceived, mixed-up logic I have ever seen. I always believed that any lawyer in a court of law not only had to follow the law but also had to be logical in any dealings with the law. But now I know better.

I find this terrifying. Had this been approved by a judge, why would any prosecutor have to deal with logical arguments when charging someone with a crime ever again? Why not just make something up and call it probable cause? Why not take the most innocent statement and call it proof of intent?

What is even more terrifying is that this really does happen.

And, what an insult to any prosecutor who has a desire to practice their profession by interpreting the law as written, by respecting a citizen's right to constitutional protection, by acting in a fair, legal, moral, and honest way. There must be prosecutors like that in the Waukesha County Department of Justice. If so, how do they feel and think about the type of behavior that gets promoted?

My case can be classified as small and insignificant. Certainly not to me but compared to high-profile cases. These high-profile cases (and low-profile cases), however, are representative of most of what happened to me and what caused me to wake up and realize that what The Center for Prosecutor Integrity reports in their white paper is true—prosecutor misconduct *is* an epidemic.

I Couldn't Resist

As I was writing about this trip to "Legal LaLa Land," my mind drifted back to an experience I had while working on my master's degree at the University of Wisconsin – Milwaukee in the mid-1970s.

I had an appointment with a professor who never showed up in his office at the appointed time or for fifteen minutes after, the amount of time I waited. The next day, I asked him why he missed our appointment. He replied that he had astro-projected his body to Mars and didn't get back on time. ("They" were unattached to reality even way back then!)

A vision popped into my mind (and with my tongue in my cheek once again). I could see these two prosecutors skipping into a field hand-in-hand, old car antennas glued to headbands they were wearing, and astro-projecting their bodies to the planet Asinine. That must have been where they got probable cause for this charge because there ain't no logic like what they used on planet Earth!

At various times in these years since those criminal charges, I asked myself how my case ever got as far as it did.

First, the DA had to have known that there wasn't a legal reason for one of these criminal charges, yet alone two. I read numerous stories about innocent people charged criminally when there wasn't a crime committed, yet many of them were convicted and jailed. I will be including some of those people in Chapter 11.

When I discovered that these Waukesha, WI prosecutors were not the only ones who had turned legal logic into an oxymoron, I realized how far our justice system had strayed from justice.

Now off to court we go again…with the facts.

The "facts" as presented by the prosecutors which establish the two elements to prove legal probable cause for a charge of criminal disorderly conduct:

1. Mens Rea (intent – a guilty mind – criminal intent)

I intentionally forgot my firearm in the bathroom with evil intent fully knowing that I was committing the crime of Disorderly Conduct.

  2. The causing of a disturbance

Multiple news stories proved that the community was outraged.

And the facts as presented by the defense attorney:

The criminal charge of disorderly conduct fails to establish the essential facts that a crime was committed as required by law.

Notes Chapter 7

1   "Probable cause," The Legal Dictionary, https://legal-dictionary.thefreedictionary.com/probable+cause

2   "Criminal law," The Free Dictionary, https://legal-dictionary.thefreedictionary.com/Criminal+Law

Generally, two elements are required in order to find a person guilty of a crime: an overt criminal act and criminal intent (mens rea). The requirement of an overt act is fulfilled when the defendant purposely, knowingly, or recklessly does something prohibited by law—that is, when a person consciously engages in certain conduct or to cause a particular result. To act knowingly means to do so voluntarily and deliberately, and not owing to mistake or some other innocent reason. An act is reckless when a person knows of an unjustifiable risk and consciously disregards it. Ordinarily, a person cannot be convicted of a crime unless he or she is aware of all the facts that make his or her conduct criminal. The reality is that prosecutors can take any law and twist it to fit their personal, professional and/or political agenda.

3   "Precedent," Law.com, https://dictionary.law.com/Default.aspx?selected=1573

4   "Precedent," Upcounsel, https://www.upcounsel.com/legal-def-precedent

5   *City of Oak Creek v. King*

Ironically, there was real evidence of community outrage regarding The Prosecutor's "bogus" criminal charge against me.

After the public condemnation to the charge of Disorderly Conduct was released by Wisconsin Carry, there were, reportedly, hundreds of letters, emails, and phone calls to the DA's office objecting to that charge by The Prosecutor.

That was provable community outrage.

Who charges a prosecutor with a crime based on her own "factual" Probable Cause for charging me with a crime?

Chapter 8

Is This a Court of Law Or...?

March 3, 2015

In retrospect, it was almost like a magic show. As in all prestidigitation, what is really going on must be kept hidden from those attending the show. The audience sits in eager anticipation. The accused's supporters, about a dozen, are chatting among themselves.

The criminally accused sits at a front table with her attorney. She is unusually quiet for one who is alleged to be guilty of disorderly conduct. Remember that she has been criminally accused of being violent, abusive, indecent, profane, boisterous, and unreasonably loud. (Doing all that without even being present at the scene where the alleged disorderly conduct occurred is, in itself, a feat of magic.) She and her attorney chat in whispers.

The prosecutor and the junior prosecutor may be discussing their attack on the grandmother who, in a twenty-page document of "probable cause," is alleged to have intentionally caused a disturbance which upset an entire community because of newspaper articles. Another feat of magic performed by Granny, herself. How powerful she must be to cause the media to write fact-challenged, biased stories that enraged an entire community.

Judge Lee S. Dreyfus Jr. walks in, the curtain is raised so to speak, everyone stands, and it begins.

The prosecutor's sleight of hand and stealth movements are dazzlingly distracting. She begins to show her skills: She brilliantly corrects the defense attorney's ghastly mistake (he initially quoted the wrong Statute number) and proudly announces that the junior prosecutor wrote the entire twenty-page probable cause document. The prosecutor gushes her compliments at her adoring protégé. A brilliant move in the guise of a prosecutor love fest. An aura of "why can't we all just get along" floods the courtroom.

She's done it! She's distracted everyone from the real reason we are here. That real reason is the fact that the law written by the legislative body of our government was wholly ignored by the DA and by the prosecutor who has been promoted from assistant district attorney to deputy district attorney as of February 2015.

Did she distract everyone from the real reason, the legality of this charge?

The defense attorney wasn't distracted. In Attorney Grieve's motion to dismiss as well as in his oral argument before the court, all he wrote and said is legally correct as well as logical. There were no facts established that the issuing of a criminal charge was justifiable.

Remember, our two savvy solicitors stated that the requirement for mens rea in a criminal disorderly charge had been met.

They proclaimed as fact, in their twenty-page brief, that I knew that when I "intentionally forgot" my firearm, I had received "proper notice that her conduct was prohibited by law, and that someone with average intelligence would know that such conduct is prohibited." I would say that even someone with below average intelligence could discern that it isn't possible to knowingly break a law that doesn't exist.

The defense attorney's motion to dismiss as well as his oral arguments in court were legal and logical He knew and quoted the law as written. No, he wasn't deceived by the sleight of hand by the prosecutor. As it turns out, neither were my supporters, neither was I, and neither was the judge.

Observations by The Observers

I have been blessed with so many wonderful family and friends. They are bright and industrious people. Of the dozen or so people present that day was a doctor, a pastor, a paralegal, a mom home-schooling her children, two other moms who were now running businesses, a VP in a large locally based corporation, a stay-at-home mom with a part-time job, and a technical support person. Their comments after the hearing were noteworthy. One of them commented on the skill in which the prosecutor put the whole responsibility of the twenty-page probable cause document on the junior prosecutor. Several others made comments like "juvenile" and "sophomoric."

Those comments mirrored what I was thinking that day.

What struck me about the whole event was the way the junior prosecutor gazed up at the prosecutor with a smile of delight at the head-patting of approval from her mentor.

The scene that immediately popped into my mind that day was of junior high school. I pictured the adoring student who would do anything for her beloved teacher. And, the teacher who knew who to recruit if she needed something accomplished for the teacher's own reason.

The other thought I along with some of the observers was how inappropriate it was to take time in a court hearing to praise another prosecutor. This hearing was about a *real person*. I am not a piece on a game board. I am sitting in the courtroom feeling like a *thing*—a *non-person*—while the "performer" points out her beautiful assistant for helping with the act.[1]

I think we all knew that court wouldn't be like TV or a movie, but we did expect a degree of appropriateness and professionalism.

Local talk show host Vicky McKenna interviewed my attorney several times regarding my case. In the first interview, when Vicky asked Attorney Grieve if I had been used as a guinea pig in a legal experiment, he said, "Yes." In a following appearance on her show, he made the statement himself that I had been a legal guinea pig.[2]

When we consider what was said by the prosecution via the transcripts of the hearings and their twenty-page brief objecting to dismissing the charge, it becomes quite apparent how convoluted was the entire case of the prosecution.

As I have written, I have all the transcripts of all the hearings.

Written in the transcript of the March 3, 2015 hearing, the prosecutor said: "There is no criminal intent in a disorderly conduct statute." At another point in the transcript of that hearing, the prosecutor said: "We aren't saying that she intentionally left the gun in the bathroom. I don't believe that to be true. I think it was an accident."

WHAT? Then why did the junior prosecutor, with the oversight of the prosecutor, bother to pen all those pages to "prove" that my act was intentional? Why would these prosecutors bother to establish mens rea—intent—if they are stating that there isn't an intent requirement in the disorderly conduct statute? Even more curious, why—after writing a twenty-page report citing cases as precedent to establish that I knew I was committing a crime—state that there isn't an intent requirement in the law? Even more confusing is the prosecutor saying that she believes forgetting my gun was an accident and that it wasn't done with intent.

This is almost like a surgeon saying that there is no medical indication that surgery is needed, but we are going to do surgery anyway because we, the surgeons, contend that surgery is needed, so we want permission to do surgery because we think that surgery should be performed, even though there is no medical indication that surgery is needed. Anyway, if this doesn't work out, we have legal immunity from any consequences.

Well, it looks like we may have another example of Unicorn Logic:

Defense Attorney: "Prosecutor _______, in your twenty-page brief you stated that you had sufficient evidence to prove intent (mens rea). You could prove that my client 'forgot' her firearm on purpose and, as mens rea means, with criminal intent.

Then, today, you state the same thing that you wrote but also say that you don't think my client left her gun in the bathroom on purpose. You believe it was an accident. Those two statements are mutually exclusive. That doesn't make sense."

Prosecutor: "What difference does that make?"

Defense Attorney: "What difference does it make? That's like a judge giving a pronouncing a verdict of guilty and not guilty at the same time."

Prosecutor: "That's ridiculous. That doesn't make any sense."

Defense Attorney: "How is that any different from what you said?"

Prosecutor: "It's different because we don't have to make sense."

Junior Prosecutor: "That's right, we're legally immune from having to make sense."

Defense Attorney: "Your Honor, could we have…"

Judge: "I know, you want a twenty-minute break so you can go outside to scream and kick the side of the building."

Defense Attorney: "No, I had to find another way to deal with extreme frustration. The last time the prosecutors tried to charge me with criminal disorderly conduct. Good thing you were with me, Your Honor."

The judge is apparently expected to view that as a legal reason for a criminal charge, i.e., we've established intent even though the crime doesn't require intent and we don't think this was an intentional act anyway.

As is typical, Judge Dreyfus took it under advisement and set another court date.

On March 31, 2015, Case Dismissed Again

Again, I appeared with my attorney and some supporters. Judge Dreyfus made a ruling. He:

1. Agreed with Judge Carter's decision saying it was correct—i.e., no probable cause in the first criminal charge.
2. This was not intentional on the defendant's part. It may have been negligent, but not to the point of criminal—no probable cause.
3. Judge Dreyfus also commented to the prosecutor that if she wanted to make law, go to the legislature.

Case dismissed for the second time. In both criminal charges the prosecutor did not have a probable cause, i.e., no legal reason for a criminal charge. Judge Dreyfus used the law as written along with reason and logic and dismissed the case as no probable cause. It is noteworthy that in his dismissal, Judge Dreyfus commented that it is the *legislature* that makes law.

I thank God for two judges—Judge Carter and Judge Dreyfus— who put aside personal bias (if there was any) and personal opinion (if there was any) and ruled by respecting the separation of powers and the rule of law.

Yet, although neither criminal charge was defensible as well as officially pronounced by two judges to have no probable cause, the prosecutor had three years from that date to charge me again.

When asked by my attorney if the prosecutor was going to charge me for the third time, she replied that she would, but she couldn't think of anything with which to charge me. (This could be considered hearsay, I suppose, but I didn't have any reason to not believe my attorney. And I knew about this prosecutor taking one woman back to court *four* times with criminal charges, so it wasn't outside the realm of possibility.)

If she charged me for a third time, the prosecutor would have nothing to lose regardless of what she did. The only people that would suffer are the innocent target and the taxpayers. And, remember, she had three years to "dream up" another charge. (Those three years were up on March 3, 2018—what a relief when that date passed.)

Think about it: It's not about the law as written by the Legislative Branch of government, it was about what she could contrive. It was about her.

It was not about the damage done to one of the citizens she was hired to serve, not about the law, not about the rule of law, not about the Constitution, not about the overcrowded court calendar or the cost to the taxpayers. It was about the prosecutor and what she wanted.

Remember, she stated the reason for issuing the second (illegitimate) criminal charge herself: The "facts" troubled her. Was this the original intent for the Department of Justice? Was this what was established for the protection of the citizens?

Was America, the home of the free, created with the intent that prosecutors in the Department of Justice were free to issue criminal charges based on their own personal, professional, and/or political purposes? Should prosecutors be legally able to charge someone with a crime because the prosecutor is personally "troubled"?

No.

However, based on my personal experience and my research,

that is precisely what is happening all over this country and at every level of the DOJ—federal, state, and county.

Prosecutors were given arbitrary, unrestricted, absolute, and unlimited power. They legally have that power because they are virtually immune from any consequences, any accountability regardless of their actions. Prosecutors are not restricted by the Constitution, by the law, by ethics, or by anything else. Of course, they are supposed to be controlled and abide by all those safeguards for the citizen. They frequently are not. Rarely to never will anyone hold them accountable. And, they know it.

Yes, there are laws—such as the Brady Law, which states that it is a crime for a prosecutor to hide information from the defense that could prove a defendant innocent (exculpatory evidence). There are ethical rules for prosecutors established by the ABA and individual states.

So, why aren't they held accountable? Because the people charged to hold them accountable, to levy consequences for prosecutors who break the law or are guilty of misconduct, refuse to hold them accountable.

As Sean Hannity once commented: *What do we do when the people who are charged with holding others accountable refuse to do so?*

American Bar Association Standard 3-1.2

Functions and Duties of the Prosecutor

(b) The primary duty of the prosecutor is to seek justice within the bounds of the law, not merely to convict.

Of course, I was relieved when another criminal charge had been dismissed. There were hugs and smiles from family and friends… but…

This Isn't Over for Me

Along with the relief, smiles, and delight, I knew it wasn't over. It wasn't over, even after my second "not guilty" charge, because the prosecutor could charge me again. And regardless if that happened or not, it wasn't over because I couldn't walk away and forget all that I had learned. I knew others had and would experience that special kind of hell that the falsely accused suffer.

I knew that too many prosecutors would continue to use innocent people for their own purposes and agendas. And I knew that each and every one of the prosecutors who did so would walk away unscathed. Even though I had also learned that getting justice from the criminal justice system was basically impossible, I had to try.

Since it appears that one of the "facts" that the prosecutor used to establish probable cause for a criminal charge was "the media got this," let's examine the media's reporting on this.

Notes Chapter 8

1   What a stunning example of trickle-down Misconduct. The Jr. Prosecutor did what she did because that was what was taught and modeled to her by The Prosecutor. I remember feeling sorry for the Jr. Prosecutor. She deserved to be taught and modeled the law as written, ethical and moral actions, and carrying out her responsibilities in the best interest of the citizen. Instead her assignment, by The Prosecutor, was to attempt to fit, twist, and spin something that was not a crime into a crime so The Prosecutor could score a win. I identified with this young woman. We both got used.

2   Vicki McKenna. *The Vicki McKenna Show.*

Chapter 9

The Media—Got Bias?

Reporter Jonah Kaplan

In 2013, Poynter Institute—cited on its website as "the world's most influential school for journalists" with the goal to "prepare journalists worldwide to…promote honest information in the marketplace of ideas"[1]—created a list of Guiding Principles for Journalists.

Seek truth and report it as fully as possible.

Be honest, fair and courageous in gathering, reporting and interpreting information.

Engage community as an end, rather than as a means.

- Seek out and disseminate competing perspectives without being unduly influenced by those who would use their power or position counter to the public interest.

- Seek publishing alternatives that minimize the harm that results from your actions and be compassionate and empathetic toward those affected by your work.

- Ethical journalism treats sources, subjects, colleagues and members of the public as human beings deserving of respect not merely as a means to your journalistic ends. Seek publishing alternatives that minimize the harm that results from your actions and be compassionate and empathetic toward those affected by your work Be compassionate for those affected by your actions.[2]

Similar principles for journalists are found in The Code of Ethics by the Society of Professional Journalists:

Minimize Harm

- Ethical journalism treats sources, subjects, colleagues and members of the public as human beings deserving of respect.

Journalists should:

- Balance the public's need for information against potential harm or discomfort. Pursuit of the news is not a license for arrogance or undue intrusiveness.[3]

Jonah was the reporter who attended and reported after the initial hearing by the court commissioner for the first criminal charge. There was some initial minor "misreporting" in his pre-court video, which appeared on Channel 4 (NBC affiliate) that evening.

It was after the court hearing that "seek[ing] truth and report[ing] it as fully as possible" as well as "minimiz [ing] harm" was not any part of Mr. Kaplan's reporting, in my opinion. After I came out of a room where I had been subjected to the humiliating process of fingerprinting and a mug shot, there was Jonah Kaplan along with his cameraman. I had to sign some papers, and in the process of doing so, my husband attempted to block me from the camera.

Even though Jonah and the cameraman were quite far away, Jonah said, to the viewing audience, that I was laughing and joking with my husband. Nothing could have been further from the truth. The woman behind the counter where I was signing the papers, seemingly having seen how devastated I was, had said something kind to me and I smiled.

When I saw Jonah's report on the news that I was laughing and joking, my first thought was that this man, Jonah Kaplan, doesn't know me. He has no idea as to my character, as to my love for children, my self-responsible attitude, my difficulties, my successes, my failures and what I did about them—he knew nothing.

Why would Mr. Jonah Kaplan say something so far-fetched? I believe that it was bias. My profile doesn't fit the political beliefs of the mainstream media, and neither does my Second Amendment standpoint. Someone like me had to be made to look like an evil person who would harm children and then laugh about it.

This reckless reporting, seemingly based on assumptions that he made about me based on my profile, assassinated my character by interpreting an act as being malicious when, in fact, it was a response to a kind and caring remark made to me by an employee of the Department of Justice.

Of course, it didn't stop there. Reporter Jonah Kaplan and his cameraman followed me down the hall asking me questions equivalent to: "Did leave your gun on purpose in order to harm children?" Those are the kinds of questions that, no matter how they are answered, make the media target look guilty because that is what the reporter wants regardless of the truth.

My attorney gave me the advice that every attorney gives: Do not say one word to the media.

Previously I would look at people who wouldn't answer a reporter's question as obviously being guilty. I always thought, just as I was manipulated to think, that the person was guilty. I will never assume that again and fall for the brainwashing of the media.

Then, as the cameraman followed behind reporter Jonah Kaplan, the cameraman shoved my then seventy-six-year-old husband out of his way and yelled, "Don't touch me." Later, we learned that this cameraman had used that same bullying tactic before. It occurred to me that if "something could have" is probable cause for a criminal charge, that cameraman needed to be charged with endangering safety.

Jonah, from the bit of research I did, is a practicing Jew. I am a Biblical Christian. We are both familiar with the Ten Commandments. Both of us need to not "be a false witness." Numerous other parts of the Old Testament and New Testament talk about gossip, lies, false testimony.

"Telling lies about others is as harmful as hitting them with an ax, wounding them with a sword, or shooting them with a sharp arrow."

Proverbs 25:18

There is that old saying: "The pen is mightier than the sword." It sure felt like journalist Jonah Kaplan aimed his weapon of words right at me. His misrepresentation of me certainly appeared to have been done purposely and irresponsibly. His words harmed.

My unintentional, much-regretted action didn't harm anyone.

Politically Promoted, Permitted, and Protected Profiling

It seems reasonably obvious that the mainstream media can practice politically protected, permitted, and even politically promoted profiling…if they do it to the "right" people.

When the Media Research Center started in 1987, only 25% *of Americans thought the media were liberal.* ***Today, 90%*** ***of Americans know the press is biased.***

For example, Judge Kavanaugh. The concept of "innocent until proven guilty" has been turned upside down. Watching the mainstream media reports as well as the actions of protesters, Judge

Kavanaugh was deemed guilty regardless of the facts. As the facts emerged, the charges were untrue unfounded. However, they will be believed anyway.

I maintain that the mainstream left-leaning media has always presented the politically incorrect as guilty until proven innocent. And, even if they are proven innocent, that person will still be considered guilty.

Depending on who you are, the media will either protect you, neglect to report about the incident, or use words and phrases to "help" their readers convict you regardless of evidence and truth. In my research, I found instances in which it appeared that the media often played a role in decisions made by the Department of Justice. The manner in which the person and incident were handled by the media mattered.

It was evident that the mainstream media could never have demonized, vilified, and dehumanized me had I not been born and made decisions that are currently "politically incorrect." Change my race, change my faith, change the place of worship, and the mainstream media would have been far too afraid to have done to someone who is currently "politically correct," as they did to me.

In fact, only months after my incident, a mother left her two young children in a car alone. In the unlocked glove compartment was a loaded gun.

> MILWAUKEE —The mother of a 3-year-old boy who accidentally shot himself with her gun will not be charged.
>
> (Name of child) was shot in the head May 3. The district attorney decided his mother didn't break the law.
>
> A written decision from the district attorney explained that while the mom left her gun in a place her son was able to find it, it doesn't rise to child neglect.

The district attorney decided that there was no legal expectation it would be found by a child when the loaded gun was placed in the glove compartment because there weren't any kids around the car at the time who saw her do it.[4]

I agree that this woman should not be charged with a crime although she did commit one. In this case, mercy is required. She will live with this for the rest of her life. The 2014 article stated that the boy was "doing much better at the hospital, and they are hoping he'll be home soon."[4]

The media was totally compassionate in this case. That's the point.

Let's compare the two incidences regarding how each woman was treated by the mainstream media:

Granny's Case	Other Case
Media demonizes	Media compassionate
Gun left unintentionally	Gun placed in the unlocked glove compartment
No children in the area	Young children left alone in the car
Nothing happened	Three-year-old shot himself

What's the difference that made the media's portrayal of these two cases dramatically different? The significant difference between the two of us is race.

Now, before the typical "racist," 'bigot," "homophobe," "xenophobe," the phobe du jour, or any other phobe still to be invented arises, I am very aware that in another time, it would have been her race that would have been demonized, vilified, and dehumanized.

Turnabout is not fair play. Hurting another person because you were hurt only brings on more revenge and more hurt.

In our current culture of who it is okay to hate, hurt, and humiliate, what if this mother had my profile? What if she were a Caucasian woman whose car was parked outside of a mega-Christian church while two young children were left alone in the car with a gun in an unlocked glove compartment and one of those children shot himself?

For her sake, I thank God that she didn't have my profile. The shame and humiliation that was heaped on me would doubtlessly have been heaped on her. I can only imagine the massive emotional damage to this woman—who was already doubtless steeped in self-blame, regret, and guilt—if the media would have done to her what they did to me.

I understand mercy in a case like that! Yet, if that woman had my profile, I doubt that the mainstream media would have treated her as compassionately as they did. I cannot help but believe that if this woman had my profile the mainstream media would have assassinated her character and misrepresented her personhood just as they did to me.

The media demonized and vilified me although, according to the law, I did not commit a crime and, not only that, no one was hurt. My politically incorrect profile resulted in the media treating me as if I were guilty of whatever they decided to lead people into believing.

Aren't News Reports Supposed to be Unbiased?

Bias is an unfair personal opinion that influences your judgment, especially one that is preconceived or unreasoned.[5] In news reporting, "objectivity means that...reporters don't convey their own feelings, biases or prejudices in their stories. They accomplish this by writing stories using language that is neutral and avoids characterizing people or institutions in ways good or bad. ... One trap beginning reporters fall into is the frequent use of adjectives.

Adjectives can easily convey one's feelings about a subject."[6] I would say that this is not just the trap of the beginning reporters. It certainly seems to be the modus operandi of the majority of mainstream media reporters.

There were similar statements concerning my case from several reporters. I hesitate to name any one reporter regarding the following because I am concerned that others wrote or said similar things.

The following statements in various forms were from several different reporters:

- That I had declined to answer questions from reporters.

Attorneys advise their clients not to talk to the media and, as I stated earlier, certainly mine did. In my trusting naiveté, I would have spoken to them. Once I started reading and hearing the twisting, the bias, and the misinformation, I was beyond grateful that my attorney had sternly warned me not to talk with them. Being charged as a criminal is nightmare enough. But the local mainstream media engaging in biased reporting—and its ability to pick and choose whose character they will assassinate based on profiling—is alarming.

- That same day an (unnamed) event had been going on in the same area of the church.

(Unnamed) is a service where parents can bring their first through fifth grade or internet schooled kids for classes and fellowship.

- That there were children in a room nearby to that bathroom.

The facts: First, (unnamed) is not held in the same area of the church—it is held on the opposite side of the building. The building is vast. The other side of the building is far removed from that bathroom.

Even if there were children still attending (unnamed), it is held in an area nowhere near that bathroom. Classes for children have bathrooms near their classrooms. If any child needed to use the bathroom from that class, there is a bigger, newer bathroom within steps of where (unnamed) was being held. I don't know why any child would walk to the opposite side of the building to use any other bathroom than the one right next to where the class had been held.

In fact, as you may remember, the witness who was questioned by the police that day also reported that there were no children around that bathroom during the time my firearm was there. The very young children have bathrooms right in their classrooms and doors are locked so a toddler, for example, can't get out unnoticed. In the over thirty years that I had attended that church, there has never, *never* been a class of girls across the hall from that bathroom.

That day, I left the church later than usual. There were very few people or children present at that time. That, no doubt, is why the man who took the firearm from the woman who found it said that no one was endangered.

- That the gun did not have a safety; the safety was not on.

That firearm, the Ruger 380, does have a safety feature. As I was informed when I purchased the gun, the safety is in the trigger pull. The trigger pull on that firearm is very long and difficult.

"Like many other semi-automatic pistols on the market, it has a safety integrated into the trigger, or if you prefer, a 'trigger in the trigger.'"

Dick Williams, *Shooting Illustrated*

"Squeezing the trigger is not much better and yields a long pull with a longer reset. Not quite as bad as a kick start on a Harley Davidson."

Mike Searson, *Ammoland*

"The LCP has a long, stiff trigger that is intended to reduce the chance of an accidental discharge."

Glenda Wagner, *The Gearhunt*

"The trigger pull is double action (long) but I like this as a feature in my concealed carry pistol because when stress is high, an accidental discharge with a light trigger would be a bad thing."

Carrie Lightfoot, *The Well-Armed Woman*

Apparently, a few words from the police report—which was factual—and the imagination of the reporters took over. Embellishments, I would assume, to make the story far scarier, turned fact into fiction. There was no evidence to back up what most of these reporters wrote. There apparently was not an effort to find evidence to prove what they reported. What they reported to the reading public as fact was not fact.

Of course, my reputation for doing what so many others have done is further destroyed. From a sentence of fact, the drama of embellishment made a far "better" story, frightened more people at that church and caused more hurt to a person—me.

The Milwaukee Journal Sentinel Legal Reporter

Bruce Vielmetti is the identified legal reporter for the *Journal Sentinel*. As a legal reporter, one would assume he is factual—indeed, no bias would be present in a story written by a legal reporter. Sometimes it is just one word that establishes not only a bias, but a rather obvious attempt to affect public opinion, i.e., to view something or someone as the reporter wants you to.

Here are two examples of his reporting:

Susan Hitchler, 67, beat the initial charge of negligent handling of a weapon when a Waukesha County judge...[7]

For the 2nd time, a woman who left a gun in church restroom beats charge.[8]

I don't know how anyone could not draw conclusions from the use of the word "beat." Doesn't that word connote "getting away with" committing a crime? The choice of that word certainly would not lead anyone to the truth. As the legal reporter, I would assume that Mr. Vielmetti knows what the legal truth was about those two criminal charges. I would assume that he knows what it means when a criminal charge is dismissed under "no probable cause." The facts don't fit what a word like "beat" leads people to believe about me or any other innocent person. What that word "beat" does is to manipulate the public mind to a biased opinion of that person. That isn't a factual, neutral, or unbiased report.

That word, used in that context, is loaded.

Instead, wouldn't it have been a real public service to report the legal reason for dismissal? What an opportunity to educate the public on legal issues. To understand what probable cause and due process means and why these things were established for the safety of the citizens of America.

What if Bruce Vielmetti had used my case to define the rule of law and how it was not followed in my case? He could have also described the constitutional rights that were violated and explained why the Fourth and Fifth Amendments are so crucial to the safety and protection of the citizens of our country.

The DA and the Media

In at least one case, the DA did not issue any criminal charges to the person who had left a gun in a public place. So why issue criminal charges to one person but not to another? Especially when the written law states so clearly, so unambiguously that there was not a crime committed. The DA had stated, in writing, that he follows the rule of law.

The American Bar Associations rules for interacting with the media as a prosecutor:

> *Model Rule 3.8(f) also imposes responsibilities on a prosecutor regarding publicity. This provision has two focal points: statements that could increase public condemnation and the exercise of reasonable care to control public comments by others working with the prosecutor.*

The DA said what's most concerning to him, in this case was that there was a Bible study group in a nearby room. There was not. The DA is familiar with that church, yet it seems as if he took his "facts" from the mainstream media reports, as seemingly did the prosecutor.

I have no evidence that either the DA or the prosecutor did due diligence regarding visiting the church and finding out exactly what happened, where the children were if there were children still present at that time, and the details of how long the gun was there, and so on. My attorney did.

The DA went on to say via the media: "It's a small gun. They could almost look toyish to someone."[9] Assuming children were nearby—which was not true—and combining that with the statement "it could almost look 'toyish' to someone" could easily increase public condemnation of someone being charged with a crime even if that person is innocent.

Whether or not the DA's statements increased public condemnation of me didn't matter. That had already been done simply by his appearing and commenting at all. The DA talking with the media and essentially giving his blessing on a criminal charge not supported by law was all that was needed for the charge to be considered legitimate and for me to be portrayed as a criminal.

So why did the DA decide to comment? Again, numerous people said to me that the criminal charge was "political." Their reasons for saying that? The DA was running for attorney general.

As this began to sink in, it made sense. The media, as opposed to an incident where a child really did get injured, took my case and embellished it beyond the facts of the actual event. We have a district attorney running for job of top cop, i.e., attorney general. I suppose he had to look "tough on crime."

Speaking truth to the media in view of the written law and the life of a citizen would have been fair and right. Or, the wiser approach would be not to speak to the media at all. A DA will often take that option so as not to lead to the pre-judgement of the person.

But never mind the facts. Never mind that Granny has no criminal record. Ignore that there was no criminal intent present. Ignore the fact that nothing happened. It was all about the optics. Tossing someone under the bus for the sake of the optics—well, that's life.

> *"Everything is at stake when a citizen becomes the target of a criminal investigation: liberty, reputation, assets, family, and legacy. An allegation that a citizen has committed a crime…can have devastating reputational consequences to the citizen with his or her family and friends and within the larger social and business community in which the citizen makes his or her life and livelihood."*

Martin and Associates website, Actions
for Wrongful Charge or Conviction

One Last Look at the Profiling and Bias of the Mainstream Media

Extreme bias and profiling were evident in the case of the Covington Catholic School young men. The mainstream media took one picture: a young man smiling at an Indian man. That one picture led the mainstream media to:

> *"…viciously maligned a group of Catholic teens who'd attended the March for Life in Washington, D.C., causing them to endure scorn, character assassination, and even threats to their safety."*
>
> Duke Selwyn, "Media Shamelessly Frame Covington Kids for Scorn and Abuse"

Of course, when all the pictures and the videos were finally revealed by other sources outside the mainstream media, the truth was revealed.

So, why would the mainstream media fabricate a vicious fake story about a teenage boy?

He was wearing a politically incorrect hat.

I understand the pain of having your character assassinated in order to make "good reading." What I found is that the "holier than thou" relished this kind of news. In the comments section of the newspaper articles about my case, several remarks to me personally—I could almost see them mount their high horses, look down their noses, and write or speak derisive comments about me or directly to me. I can certainly understand why these children—and they *are* children—were afraid for their safety.

Got bias, mainstream media?

> *"Whoever controls the media, controls the mind."*
>
> Jim Morrison

Notes Chapter 9

1   "Mission & Vision," Poynter Institute, https://www.poynter.org/mission-vision/

2   Kelly McBride, "The New Ethics of Journalism: About this blog," The Poynter Institute, https://www.poynter.org/reporting-editing/2013/about-this-blog/

3   Society of Professional Journalists Code of Ethics, https://www.spj.org/ethicscode.asp

4   Nick Bohr, "DA won't charge mother after son shot himself with her gun," WISN.com, May 23, 2014, https://www.wisn.com/article/da-won-t-charge-mother-after-son-shot-himself-with-her-gun/6321555

5   "Bias," Dictionary.com, https://www.dictionary.com/browse/biases

6   Tony Rogers, "Objectivity and Fairness in Journalism," ThoughtCo, June 28, 2018, https://www.thoughtco.com/objectivity-and-fairness-2073726

7   Bruce Vielmetti, "Woman who left gun in Brookfield church faces new charge," *Journal Sentinel*, November 28, 2014, http://archive.jsonline.com/news/crime/woman-who-left-gun-in-brookfield-church-faces-new-charge-b99399141z1-284156741.html/

8   Bruce Vielmetti, "For 2nd time, woman who left gun in church restroom beats charge," *Journal Sentinel*, March 31, 2015, http://archive.jsonline.com/newswatch/298194631.html

9   Christina Palladino, "Woman charged after leaving loaded gun inside church," WISN.com, April 28, 2014, https://www.wisn.com/article/woman-charged-after-leaving-loaded-gun-inside-church/6321130

Chapter 10

How "For the People and By the People" Has Morphed Into "For the Government and By the Government"

Violating Constitutional Rights: Due Process and Probable Cause

For this chapter, I will be your non-attorney "spokes-granny."

The good news about not being an attorney is that I had to put any "legalese" that occurred in my reading and research into language that I could understand. I also looked up the specific legal definitions of terms in the online legal dictionaries. The definitions tended to be more understandable; therefore, I hope that helps all non-attorney readers to better understand how we are losing the liberty, freedom, and protection given to us by the Constitution and the Bill of Rights. There are also legal maxims that have been used since the founding of our country to protect us.

The Fourth, Fifth, and Fourteenth Amendments to our Constitution were for the safety of the citizens. Our founders wanted to protect the citizens of this newly formed country from arbitrary and tyrannical rule. These amendments establish due process[1] and probable cause[2] as protection from arbitrary arrest, seizure of personal property, and arbitrary, unsupported, groundless prosecution by government employees of the Department of Justice.

To Review:

Due Process ("Fundamental Fairness")

1. The government must provide notice of the charges against you.

2. The government must be able to show that there is an articulated (non-vague) standard of conduct which you are accused of violating.

3. The government must provide you with an opportunity to rebut their charges against you in a meaningful way and at a meaningful time (the "hearing requirement").

4. To sustain its position for the deprivation of your liberty or property, the government must establish—at a minimum—that there is substantial and credible evidence supporting its charges.

5. The government must provide some explanation to the individual for the basis of any adverse finding.[1]

Probable cause:

Apparent facts discovered through logical inquiry that would lead a reasonable, intelligent, and prudent person to believe that an accused person has committed a crime, thereby warranting his or her prosecution. ... Probable Cause is a level of reasonable belief, based on facts that can be articulated, that is required to prosecute a person in criminal court before a person can be prosecuted; the prosecutor must possess enough facts that would lead a reasonable person to believe the claim or charge is true. ... The Probable Cause standard is more important in Criminal Law than it is in Civil Law.[2]

The legislative body of our government makes law, and the judicial body's responsibility is to interpret it and apply it. The separation of powers, once again, was instituted for the safety of the citizen. The reason was so that not one power—executive, legislative, or judicial—could obtain absolute, arbitrary, and tyrannical power. The separation provided checks and balances. Quite frankly, it was ingenious. No country had ever been set up like America.

Let's look specifically at my case.

There will be some repetition of information already presented. Sometimes seeing the same information in a different context assists in understanding the overall message—the bigger picture—much better.

First, in my case, due process was ignored. My personal property was taken and held without any evidence that a crime had been committed.

Even after the first charge was dismissed, the prosecutor instructed the police not to return my firearm. She had no constitutional right to do that. That was seizing personal property for no legal reason but simply because of an arbitrary decision by a government employee. The only probable cause that the prosecutor ever verbalized to me regarding her first criminal charge was that "the media got this" and she needed to "send a message to the community." What was the message? I have no idea.

In issuing the second criminal charge, she stated that it "continued to bother her."

A prosecutor must possess enough facts that would lead a reasonable person to believe that the criminal charge is warranted. The facts and only the facts provide probable cause for a criminal charge.

Due process is violated as well as probable cause far too often and in far too many cases by our present-day Department of Justice.

I was fortunate—I believe blessed—to have two judges, Waukesha County judges, Judge Carter and Judge Dreyfus, who did understand and abide by the Constitution, the rule of law, and the separation of powers.

"The prosecutor has more control over life, liberty, and reputation than any other person in America. His discretion is tremendous… While the prosecutor at his best is one of the most beneficent forces in our society, when he acts from malice or other base motives; he is one of the worst."

Former U.S. Attorney General Robert Jackson

There was not one of the legally educated, trained, and licensed persons in the Department of Justice who gave credence to the law that described in perfect detail what would make my unintentional act a crime.

When reading about other cases, I often wondered how those cases got as far up the line in the Department of Justice as they did. I wonder no longer.

How could the prosecutor, who got a promotion, and the DA who was running for attorney general not have known about Wisconsin State Statute 948.55? How could they not have known that it was written law which spelled out clearly that there was no probable cause that a crime had been committed?

The DA, by the way did become our attorney general. However, in the 2018 election, he lost. Ironically, he was appointed to a judgeship—in Waukesha County criminal court.

I cannot help but wonder how, as a judge, the DA would have ruled in my case.

Mens Rea (Criminal Intent)

It might be a surprise to learn that it is the God of the Bible who established the long-held legal requirement of intent for any act to be a crime. In other words, a person needed to have a guilty mind. The person had to know that something is a crime, that their action was wrong, and intentionally do it anyway.

Ultimate wisdom—the God of the Bible, knowing that we are

imperfect humans, established the necessity for intent for an action to be a crime. Therefore, something done by accident without any criminal intent, is not a crime.

For example, if someone killed another by accident, i.e., had no intention of causing the death of that person, God had cities where these people could go and be safe from harm by others intent on revenge. God, knowing we are human and subject to error, subject to unintentional acts, made sure that people who never had a "criminal" intent were not punished for something that was done unintentionally.

> *"Anyone who strikes a man and kills him shall surely be put
> to death. However, if he does not do it intentionally, but God
> lets it happen, he is to flee to a place I will designate."*

Exodus 21:12-13

> *"But if without hostility someone suddenly shoves another or throws
> something at him unintentionally or, without seeing him, drops a stone
> on him that could kill him, and he dies, then since he was not his
> enemy and he did not intend to harm him, the assembly must judge
> between him and the avenger of blood according to these regulations.
> The assembly must protect the one accused of murder from the avenger
> of blood and send him back to the city of refuge to which he fled."*

Numbers 35:22-25

From God's law came the legal requirement of mens rea.

Mens rea refers to criminal intent. The literal translation from Latin is "guilty mind." A mens rea refers to the state of mind required to convict a particular defendant of a particular crime. Basing our laws on God's meant that if there was no criminal intent, there was no crime.[3]

This is where justice and mercy can be balanced to protect us imperfect humans from being punished for an accident, i.e., something that was not done on purpose. There was no intent, no guilty mind.

So, for many years prosecutors and judges followed this rule. Not anymore.

What happened to mens rea? I have come to think that it is because convictions are what counts in the Department of Justice, ignoring mens rea has given prosecutors far more people to criminally charge in the hopes of racking up convictions. For what other purpose can an unintentional act be accepted by a court of law as being a just reason to issue a criminal charge?

Remember how this book got its title. One of our grandchildren, while doing a school assignment online, came across the mainstream media reports about his grandmother, me. He asked his dad what his grandmother had done, what crime did she commit?

When his dad told him, our grandson replied: "Well, that's really stupid. That's not a crime and Grandma didn't do it on purpose."

Amazing! It seems that this young mind thought the way ultimate wisdom thought. When someone did not mean to do something, how could it be a crime?

At age thirteen our grandson had not gone to law school. He didn't have a degree in law, and he didn't pass the Bar. Yet, he instinctively knew what was morally and ethically right. He instinctively knew that an accidental act done with no criminal intent could not and should not be a crime.

After five years of investigating and studying prosecutor misconduct, I believe that I can confidently state that prosecutors are straying far afield from what is actual crime. Is one of the reasons that our allegedly overcrowded court calendars are overcrowded because mens rea—intent, a guilty mind—is frequently ignored? Are the tax payers being burdened by paying for cases that should never have come to court in the first place?

Further, how can someone who did something accidently be rehabilitated? What positive results come from punishing someone who did something unintentionally? How is anyone taught how not to do something unintentionally—ever—in their lives?

> *"If you don't harm anyone there is no crime. This has been long standing in England and America. Therefore, it is wrong for the government to charge someone with a crime when no one was harmed. If you are going to enforce the law, you must be required to obey it."*

Judge Andrew Napolitano

The prosecutor—and the DA—must have known what mens rea is. She graduated from law school. This had to be part of her education.

Both have law degrees. Both passed the Bar.

Yet, neither of these prosecutors, with their law degrees, appeared to have the common sense of a child nor the respect for a law instituted by the Creator of the universe. Not to mention, ignoring the law as written by the Legislative Branch of our government.[4] God declared that even if someone was harmed by the unintentional act, there was no crime. But God, of course, always understood lack of any evil intent even if someone was harmed. He called the person who had no evil intent innocent.

Interestingly, the same DA who allowed me to be charged twice with a crime didn't charge the man who left a bar, fell asleep at the wheel of his car, and killed a bicyclist. The DA said he couldn't think of anything with which to charge him.

I understand mercy in a case like this. Of course, this man didn't murder the bicyclist. He didn't kill him intentionally. That man will suffer all his life. But where was the DA's mercy in a clear case of no mens rea and legislatively no crime in my case?

This gives me even more reason to believe that my criminal charges were not about the law, not about an actual crime, but about the career aspirations of two prosecutors.

That is not the United States of America that our founders

envisioned. They knew full well that a rogue, unaccountable judicial system could create an oppressive government. They were right. In fact, the Judicial Branch of government was meant to have the least power. Today, it has become evident that it has the most.

Prosecutors are the most powerful people in the criminal justice system.

"Unchecked power in the hands of prosecutors is as much a threat to our democracy as it is with any other government official, if not more."

Angela J. Davis, *The New York Times*

When these basic rights given to us are ignored, how is America any different from the tyrannical, arbitrary governments of other countries?

Anglo-American Criminal Law Was Based on God's Law

This may be a surprise, especially for those who have been exposed to rewritten history, but most of our founders were influenced by the God of the Bible. The evidence in their writings is overwhelming.[5] Because of that, much of the protections for citizens was based on God's principles and laws as written in the Bible. In fact, the idea of the separation of powers came from the Bible. In Isaiah 33:22 came the idea for the three branches of government:

"For the Lord is our judge, the Lord is our lawgiver, the Lord is our king; it is he who will save us."

Obviously, we're not God (Although some might believe that they are ☺). But when we have one branch making law, one applying written law, and one the "executive" where the buck stops, tyranny is put in check.

The idea of a representative government also came from God in Exodus 18:17–22:

> *"Moses' father-in-law replied, 'What you are doing is not good. You and these people who come to will only wear yourselves out. The work is too heavy for you; you cannot handle it alone. Listen now to me and I will give you some advice, and may God be with you. You must be the people's representative before God.' … Moses listened to his father-in-law and did everything he said. He chose capable men from all Israel and made them leaders of the people, officials over thousands, hundreds, fifties and tens."*

The United States of America was organized in a way that no government before had ever been. It was meant to give us the ability to be free from dictatorial, oppressive human rule. The separation of powers and the establishment of a representative government was unique. The founders of America took most of it straight from ultimate wisdom.

Day by day that freedom is being eroded whether you choose to believe that or not. My experience with the Department of "Justice" made me a believer.

False Witness

The Ninth Commandment is found in Exodus 20:16: "You shall not bear false witness against your neighbor." This principle includes all forms of lying. The Ninth Commandment was God's admonishment against slander and the perversion of justice.

> *"As God told Moses and the Israelites: 'You shall not circulate a false report. Do not put your hand with the wicked to be an unrighteous witness. You shall not follow a crowd to do evil; nor shall you testify in a dispute…to pervert justice.'"*

Exodus 23:1 (NKJV)

The Word is clear

> *"If a malicious witness arises to accuse a person of wrongdoing…*
> *The judges shall inquire diligently, and if the witness is a*
> *false witness and has accused his [or her] brother falsely, then*
> *you shall do to him as he had meant to do to his brother"*

Deut. 19:16–19, NKJV).

Based on God's Word, which required consequences for perverting justice, prosecutors must be held accountable for misconduct in any form. This would include, of course, perverting justice to benefit themselves.

> *"…this law should be extended to the prosecutors (and in other cases, the police and the agencies, too).* ***When they fail to "inquire diligently," but instead harbor, protect, and represent the falsehood, then by the principle of representation, they become the "malicious witness" themselves. They should pay the price also.***

Rogue prosecutors: a case example on the need for biblical accountability laws Jul 23, 2015 by Dr. Joel McDurmon

> *The bottom line is this:* ***there ought to be a solid principle of accountability for rogue,*** *or even simply unsupported but persistent, accusers in society. This includes not only liars like…, but* ***police, judges, and prosecutors who pervert justice on their own or others' behalf."***

IBID

What surprised me the most, when I began my research into prosecutor misconduct, is the fact that prosecutors are rarely to never held responsible for anything. That includes constitutional violations. That seems to be the first matter that should be checked for a criminal charge to be issued.

Speaking quite boldly, the bigger surprise is that it seems the entire system doesn't appear to care one wit about constitutional violations – due process, probable cause – or the rule of law. In fact, it is so commonplace that I doubt that anyone even knows, much less cares, about the loss of so many of the rights established to protect citizens.

In Wisconsin, district attorneys sign a document in which they swear to uphold the Constitution of the United States of America and the Constitution of the State of Wisconsin. (I have a copy of the oath sworn and signed by the DA. I also have a copy of the OK by the DA for both criminal charges that the prosecutor issued against me.)

I don't know for sure if prosecutors—who are hired, not elected—take that same oath. However, it is the responsibility of the district attorney to make sure that prosecutors in the department are acting according to the Constitution of the United States and the State of Wisconsin. The DA must take responsibility since he/she signs and OKs all criminal charges.

Notes Chapter 10

1   Doug Linder, "Procedural Due Process," Exploring Constitutional Conflicts, http://law2.umkc.edu/faculty/projects/ftrials/conlaw/proceduraldueprocess.html

2   "Probable cause," The Free Dictionary, https://legal-dictionary.thefreedictionary.com/probable+cause

3   The fact that the once well-established fundamental legal requirement for mens rea (intent) is rarely considered in the "modern day" DOJ has become evident and is disturbing to many. One example:

> "The bedrock principle of Anglo-American criminal law has always been that people must know they are doing something wrong before they can be found guilty and branded a criminal. This legal concept is known as mens rea, Latin for 'guilty mind.' The reason for this fundamental legal requirement is obvious: violations of criminal laws are serious, and before we put a fellow citizen in jail, we want to make certain that he is actually a bad person, is morally culpable for his crime, and that he deserves to go to jail. Meting out harsh punishment to those who don't even truly understand the import of their actions offends our very notion of justice. … Many of the new criminal provisions have no requirement of criminal intent, meaning that morally innocent people can (and will) receive harsh criminal penalties for otherwise innocent mistakes."
>
> Larry D. Thompson, former Deputy Attorney General of the United States, *In Criminal Trials, the "Guilty Mind" Does Matter*

4   Ignoring God's law as well as the written law would be especially problematic for a Department of Justice prosecutor who publicly affirms Christianity. The talk and the walk need to match—or it is just words?

No one is perfect (I obviously speak for myself). However, when one calls himself or herself a Christian, there needs to be an honest view of his or her actions. Character, as often has been said, is what you do when no one is looking.
A Christian knows that a dishonest, immoral, illegal act may escape human eyes and that there is the probability that no one will hold them accountable, but, as written in our Constitution: "Appealing to the Supreme Judge of the world for the rectitude of our intentions…" God will see and will fairly judge
The Founders of our Country based much of what they did and wrote on God's Word. Today, that is being denied by many. Fortunately, we can refer to sources that will give us evidence that the Founders did, indeed, base the foundation of this newly forming nation on The Word of God.

A group of contemporary political scientists embarked on an ambitious ten-year project (beginning in the early 1970's) to analyze the political writings from the Founding Era (1760-1805). Those writings were examined with the goal of isolating and identifying the specific polit-ical sources cited amidst the debates in the establishment of American government.

From the 15,000 representative writings selected, the researchers first isolated some 3,154 quotations and then documented the orig-inal sources. Baron Charles de Montesquieu a French attorney and author was the most frequently invoked political source 8.3%, from his (1748) Spirit of Laws. The second most frequently quoted was Blackstone 7.9%.

Perhaps to their amazement, what the researchers discovered:

*"[T]hat one direct source of inspiration for their ideas was cited far and away more than any other. In fact, the Founders cited this source four times more often than either Montesquieu or Blackstone and twelve times more often than Lock. What was that source? **It was the Bible-accounting for 34 percent of the direct***

quotes in the political writings of the Founding Era."

God's Law the Foundation of Free Government by Carolyn Alder

For more documentation refer to Beckman W. (2015). **Our Christian Founding Fathers: "...this is a Christian nation".** (1st edition). USA: West Bow Press. In my Bibliography

Chapter 11

In Whose Best Interest?

Both of My Charges Were Dismissed—Or Were They?

Even after the dismissal of two charges due to no probable cause, the prosecutor had three years to charge me again. This is because both of my charges were dismissed without prejudice.

A case dismissed *with* prejudice means that it is dismissed permanently—it's over and done with. The prosecutor cannot come back with another criminal charge for that person for the same act. Therefore, a case dismissed *without* prejudice means just the opposite. The prosecutor can issue a criminal charge again to the same person for that same act.

Essentially, without prejudice means that the case is dismissed without any prejudice to the prosecutor (criminal case). This means that the court believes that none of the rights or privileges of the defendant had been lost or waived. (I didn't lose any of my rights?) The dismissal without prejudice means that the decision was not made on the merits of the case. Consequently, the prosecutor can issue another criminal charge with no regard for the dismissal of the first charge.

What, exactly, were the merits of the criminal charge against me? Even more pertinent, why didn't anyone ever consider and interpret the law as written? That's what the Judicial Branch of government is charged to do. The Judicial Branch of our government, to the best of my knowledge, was never meant to attempt to find a law in order to make something into a crime which the Legislative Branch specifically decided as not being a crime?

In addition to the statute that specifically states that my unintentional action was not a crime, there is also a Wisconsin State statute that legally defines a crime:

Wisconsin State Statute 939.12:

Crime defined

> A crime is conduct which is prohibited by state law and punishable by fine or imprisonment or both.

As an "average" citizen with no formal legal training, it logically looks to me like both laws, i.e., 948.55 and 939.12, written by the Legislative Branch of government, were ignored by the Judicial Branch.

If I were a legislator, I would feel dismissed by people in the Judicial Branch of government as not being worthy of respect for me or what I was elected to do. Why write the laws at all, if they're going to be ignored?

My case was dismissed because there was no legal reason for issuing it in the first place.

Consider that:

- Even though the prosecutor either violated SCR 20:3.8 (an ethical violation, which is misconduct), or may not understand probable cause and the law as written, which makes one wonder if she is qualified to be a prosecutor.
- and/or she was stepping over the bounds of the separation of powers.
- even though my constitutional rights were violated.
- even though the law as written was ignored…

The prosecutor was not held accountable for her actions i.e. two no probable cause criminal charges, violating my constitutional rights, and ignoring the law as written. And, I have no recourse while she had three years to come up with another criminal charge.

In whose best interest?

A Prosecutor Intent on Winning
Regardless of the Written Law

"In such a case, it is not a question of discovering the commission of a crime and then looking for the man (or woman) who has committed it. It is a question of picking the man (or woman) and then searching the law books or putting investigators to work to pin some offense on him (or her)."

Paul Craig Roberts and Lawrence M. Stratton, *The Tyranny of Good Intentions*

After the first charge was dismissed due to no probable cause, the prosecutor apparently wanted to try again.

During the summer of 2014, the prosecutor reportedly had marshaled several district attorney's offices around the state as well as law students in an effort to find another statute; another written law, that would allow her to criminally charge me for the second time.

This information came from various sources. I had to promise never to reveal who, for understandable reasons. Of course, in a court of law, this would be labeled hearsay. Consequently, I want to stress that under the circumstances, it must be taken as hearsay.

However, the reason I believe that the prosecutor did so is because of the previous quote and the one below. In the books on prosecutor misconduct that I read as well as numerous articles and reports online, there were enough examples of prosecutors doing what the prosecutor allegedly did.

"Junior and senior prosecutors would sit around over beer and

Each and every time I read facts like that, I felt dismayed. Actually, horror-struck. When one group of people can do what prosecutors can do without any consequences at all, we have uncontrolled power. Absolute and unchecked power in the hands of a few people is always dangerous for the citizens of a country. All of us have our freedom and well-being at stake.

Also, consider the tax money spent on the prosecutor's persistence to get a conviction for a crime when Wisconsin State Law specifically stated that it was not a crime. How much money, how many other tax-paid employees were involved, how much time was spent by the prosecutor to "pin some offense" on me?

Remember what the prosecutor said to me in the "pre-charge" interview? She told me that it would take her "months" to decide if she was going to charge me criminally. We now know, and I assume that she must have known, that the only appropriate law (Wisconsin State Statute 948.55) for the exact circumstance specifically included the facts that would establish probable cause for a criminal charge. Nothing like that happened.

I can now take a more educated guess that if I had an attorney in that room with me, the "it would take months" would have been challenged based on my constitutional right to a speedy trial. I can also take an educated guess that with an attorney in the room, the prosecutor would never have said anything like that.

It certainly appears that far too many prosecutors have forgotten whose best interests they were hired to serve. The best interest of the citizens should be first and foremost. Not the best interest of the prosecutor.

Prosecutors have been given virtually absolute legal immunity for almost anything that they do. Rarely to never are they held accountable and face consequences. I have followed a group formed by a man who was the target, the victim of an abusive prosecutor. His organization is named It Could Happen to You (www.itcould-happen2you.org), a non-profit criminal justice reform organization dedicated to ending wrongful prosecutions/convictions, reforming bail, discovery and speedy trial laws.[1]

In one of the organization's recent email newsletters:

Vol. 5/No 375 August 1, 2018

Must Sign Legislation Creating an Oversight Commission

By Frederic Block—Federal Judge

New York Daily News, July 30, 2018

Prosecutors are responsible for holding people accountable when they violate the law, but what happens when the prosecutors are the ones who break the rules? In most instances, nothing.

For example, _______ spent 16 years in prison for a 1994 Brooklyn murder that he did not commit. His case was overturned...

As a federal judge for over two decades, the level of prosecutorial abuse and lack of accountability, in this case, has haunted
me. I presided over the civil case that ____ brought seeking
damages for the violation of his rights. While I ruled that the
city could be held liable, I was forced to dismiss the claims
against the prosecutor and the district attorney on grounds of
prosecutorial immunity.

Since then, the state and city taxpayers have paid $13 million
in settlements stemming from ______'s wrongful conviction.
The prosecutor hasn't paid a dime, nor has he been punished
at all for his egregious behavior.

We have no idea how many other cases and how much more of our
tax money has been wasted over cases that should never have been
brought to court in the first place, both in Wisconsin (most notably
the Walker John Doe) and in the entire country.

While prosecutors have virtually no consequences for their actions,
the innocent person and the taxpayers do have consequences. Let's
also consider that behavior like this is passed down from one prosecutor to the next. It is also often lauded and becomes a reason for
a promotion.

> *"Is it any wonder the misconduct doesn't stop? The incentive isn't
> there. After all, a high-profile prosecution can turn a prosecutor into a
> local celebrity…launch a political career. Even something as serious
> as 'reckless professional misconduct' merits little more than short
> suspension. Sometimes, however, misconduct merits a promotion."*

Jay Sekulow, *Undemocratic: How Unelected, Unaccountable
Bureaucrats are Stealing Your Liberty and Freedom*

The prosecutor, in my case, did get a promotion either because
of or despite the numerous seemingly ethical, constitutional, and
the rule of law violations present in my case. The prosecutor is now

in a position to officially affect (infect?) other prosecutors to follow her type of conduct as a prosecutor. As a DDA (deputy district attorney), she is in a managerial type position where she supervises and instructs ADAs (assistant district attorneys).

I Am One of Many

The more I read books, articles, papers from attorneys and judges as well as from victims of prosecutor use and abuse, the more I realized that prosecutors using innocent people for their own reasons and not for a legal reason was far bigger than I could have even imagined.

One of the most personally disturbing cases that I read was in *Licensed to Lie: Exposing Corruption in the Department of Justice* by Sidney Powell. The case of Jim B. had the most visceral effect on me. It still makes me sick when I think about what he and his family suffered because of prosecutors' selfish agendas. Attorney Powell comments that she has read more than 350 criminal trial transcripts and con-sulted on countless criminal cases. But she said, "As hard as I looked, I couldn't find a criminal offense alleged in the indictment." She went on to say that: "(the transcript) cited statutes […] but it failed to allege anything that actually constituted a crime. … Instead it cobbled together parts of different statutes to make up some kind of new crimes that didn't even make sense."

In Attorney Powell's chapter "The Longest Year," she wrote about the horrors Jim endured in prison. Tears came to my eyes for this man who never committed a crime. Not only that, but he thought that if he just told the truth, everything would be all right. The truth doesn't matter to a prosecutor whose goal is not justice.

For a while, Jim was in a cell with thirteen other people. One of Jim's cellmates was set on fire while asleep. Jim lived in fear of being attacked by other inmates and even by the guards. Jim had to shave his head and mustache because the filth and bugs were so horrendous. He was sensory deprived and degraded daily.

The prosecutor task force did everything they could to make every minute of Jim's existence as miserable and frightening as possible. While Jim and the other men in this same case who had also been convicted of "no crimes" suffered a hellish existence, the prosecutors in the task force were, as Attorney Powell wrote: "being promoted, honored, and lauded for their work."[2]

Yes, anyone can be the victim of a prosecutor even when they have not committed a crime. Just ask the "average" citizen targets of the Scott Walker John Doe case in Wisconsin.

The early-morning invasions into the private homes of these people were frighteningly like those of an all-powerful government. Like many third-world governments, the invasions were carried out devoid of any constitutional protections established for the safety and freedoms of its citizens. This nightmare, which started with unlawful and unconstitutional home invasions, which most Americans believe could never happen in America—the home of the free—did happen in America!

The harm that was done to innocent citizens was allegedly based on Milwaukee County DA John Chisholm's teacher wife's dislike and disapproval of Wisconsin Governor Scott Walker's Act 10. None of them committed a crime. Yet, they suffered through a nightmare for years because of the political agenda of Milwaukee County prosecutor John Chisholm.

The following direct quotes, reported in the National Guardian and written by David French, came from 3 of the targets of prosecutor ordered early morning raids on the private homes of innocent citizens

"THEY CAME WITH A BATTERING RAM." Said _______, "I was so afraid," she says. "I did not know what to do." She grabbed some clothes, opened the door, and dressed right in front of the police. The dogs were still frantic. "I begged and begged, 'Please don't shoot my dogs, please don't shoot my dogs, just don't shoot my dogs".

And, from my research I learned that this is not the first or only time that American Citizens have experienced what unbelievably, does happen in this country.

The harm done to these innocent people is beyond imagination. It has continued for many years and was still going on at the time of this writing.

These "victims" of a prosecutor with a political agenda never committed a crime. Yet, there are still repercussions to this day. Their personal property was seized without Due Process of Law. They are still fighting for justice. They are still fighting to have their personal property returned.[2]

By the way, John Chisholm, at the time of this writing, is still the district attorney of Milwaukee County.

"It is hard to imagine a more stupid or more dangerous way of making decisions than by putting those decisions in the hands of people who pay no price for being wrong."

Thomas Sowell

Simply because you didn't commit a crime doesn't mean that a prosecutor cannot charge you with a crime.

In the American Family Association newsletter, I recently read about a pastor who left Iran to escape persecution for his Christian faith. He is an American citizen living in California.

Pastor Ramin Parsa came to Minnesota to speak. Since he was in Minnesota, he decided to visit the Mall of America. At the mall, he started to converse with two Somali-American women. They asked him to talk to them about his faith and his conversion from Islam. Another Muslim woman overheard the conversation and reported him to mall security.

Even though the Somali women told the security officer that the conversation was welcome and requested, Pastor Parsa was arrested. When onlookers asked the Somali women what happened, they said that Pastor Parsa had been arrested because he was a Christian. Pastor Parsa was charged with trespassing.[3] He was held in the basement of the Mall for four hours while handcuffed to a metal chair. He was denied water and access to the bathroom. The Bloomingdale, MN police arrested him.[4]

That was in August of 2018. In November of 2018, he was awaiting trial, charged with Illegal Solicitation and Criminal Trespass. The state of Minnesota continued to prosecute his case, even though the Mall of America was wrong to accuse him of trespassing in the first place. Think about this. He left Iran where he was being persecuted for being a Christian and came to America, home of the free, to be persecuted for being a Christian.

On March 18, 2019 these ridiculous charges were dropped.[4] But, of course, as in all cases where there is no legal reason to charge someone with a crime, the "victim" still suffers consequences. So does the taxpayer. And, a criminal justice system that is allegedly overwhelmed adds a senseless, unnecessary burden to the courts.

Nothing is more essential to a just criminal law than making sure that the average American cannot become a criminal accidentally or inadvertently without intending to do anything unlawful or otherwise wrongful. Today, at any moment, a person can find himself facing the business end of a criminal investigation and prosecution because he has merely:

- Chosen to start small businesses and not properly filled out some paperwork required by a confusing web of federal and international law,

- Not added the right sticker to an otherwise properly shipped UPS package,

- Failed to comply with unreasonable bureaucratic interpretations of city landscaping requirements,

- Not known that it was a federal crime to cut down a certain tree on his own residential property, or

- Eaten a French fry in a public place. (A 12-year-old girl was arrested, searched and handcuffed. … Her shoelaces were removed, and she was transported in the windowless rear compartment of a police vehicle to a juvenile processing center, where she was booked, fingerprinted and detained until released to the custody of her mother, some three hours later—all for eating a single French fry in a Metrorail station.)

One Nation Under Arrest, edited by Paul Rosenzweig & Brian W. Walsh

Original Intent

"If man will not subject himself to the Ten Commandments of God, he will be made subject to the ten thousand commandments of men."

G.K. Chesterton

As we discussed in Chapter 10, our system of justice was based on God's Word. It started out with God's law. But just like the religious leaders of Jesus' day, the "government" kept adding laws upon laws and rules upon rules to the law, making it a cumbersome and onerous burden. The same is true of our justice system today.

The rejection of God's laws in favor of man's laws started in the Old Testament, in fact. Israelites wanted a king just like other nations had. God wasn't enough. They wanted human leadership, human laws, human reasoning.

Jill Briscoe (wife of Pastor Stuart Briscoe and a prolific Christian author and talented speaker in her own right) has oft said, God is a gentleman. If you keep insisting on your way, He will let you have it.

The Israelites got what they wanted - kings. Almost every one of the kings—the government they wanted—was cruel, oppressive, arbitrary and acted in their own best interest and not the best interest of their subjects. The people suffered greatly.

Sad but true, "government" like the Old Testament kings seems to forget who they were charged to serve. They begin to become more and more self-serving regardless of the harm done to those who they were to serve.

*"But criminal law does not drive criminal punishment. It would be closer to the truth to say that criminal punishment drives criminal law. The definition of crimes and defenses plays a different and much smaller role in the allocation of criminal punishment than we usually suppose. In general, the role it plays is **to empower prosecutors, who are***

__the criminal justice system's real lawmakers__. Anyone who reads criminal codes in search of a picture of what conduct leads to a prison term, or who reads sentencing rules in order to discover how severely different sorts of crimes are punished, will be seriously misled."

William J. Stuntz *The Pathological Politics of Criminal Law*

"The more corrupt the state, the more numerous the laws."

Cornelius Tacitus, historian and senator of the Roman Empire

The first step toward reform is educational and political. Since virtually everyone is affected by these issues, virtually everyone needs to become informed and motivated to act. Members of all three branches of government need to be pounded with the message that the present trend is wrong, that it is harming society, and that it is eroding trust in, and respect for, government and law.

Edited by Gene Healy *Go Directly To Jail: The Criminalization of Almost Everything*

Notes Chapter 11

1   Bill Bastuk was a victim of a district attorney in New York State. He and his wife lost their life savings over bogus charges.

It is a fact that prosecutors have legal immunity for virtually anything they do. As much as someone attempts to make a prosecutor accountable, in the vast majority of cases, that person loses and there are no consequences for the prosecutor.

One of many, many cites:

"A three-judge panel for the U.S. Court of Appeals for the 7th Circuit just issued as an important opinion (**PDF**) on absolute immunity, the policy that makes it impossible to sue prosecutors who engage in misconduct, even when that misconduct results in a wrongful conviction."

"Prosecutors at all levels of the criminal justice system enjoy this absolute immunity from lawsuits. It's a sweeping bit of judge-made law that essentially shields them from any civil liability for even egregiously bad behavior, even when said behavior results in a wrongful convictions."

"7th Circuit pokes a hole in prosecutorial immunity"
Radley Balko

2   Sidney Powell, *Licensed To Lie: Exposing Corruption in the Department of Justice* (USA: Brown Books Publishing Group, 2014).

3   Matt Kittle, "DOJ Report: Wisconsin's Infamous John Doe Was More Sinister Than First Reported," MacIver Institute, December 7, 2017, http://www.maciverinstitute.com/2017/12/doj-report-wisconsins-infamous-john-doe-was-more-sinister-than-first-reported/

The Illegal John Doe started in 2010. There was a John Doe I and II. It has been noted that there may be a secret John Doe III.

Supreme Court Decisions regarding the John Doe:
-Unconstitutional and that the investigation's prosecutor (special prosecutor Francis Schmitz) instigated a "perfect storm of wrongs" on the innocent targets. (The National Guardian calls it Wisconsin's Shame.)
-this conclusion ends the John Doe investigation because the special prosecutor's legal theory is **unsupported in either reason or law**." (Judge Gableman) (Frankly – that seems true for my case as well.)

4   Anthony Gockowski, "Charges Dropped Against Christian Pastor Arrested at Mall of America," *Tennessee Star* March 9, 2019 https://tennesseestar.com/2019/03/09/charges-dropped-against-christian-pastor-arrested-at-mall-of-america/

The mission of the American Family Association is to inform, equip, and activate individuals to strengthen the moral foundations of American culture, and give aid to the church here and abroad in its task of fulfilling the Great Commission."

www.AFA.net

"When we came out of the coffee shop, three guards were waiting for us, and they arrested me right there," Parsa told PJ Media <u>back in September</u>. "They came after me and arrested me,

Parsa told security he was a pastor. "They told me, 'We arrested pastors before,'" he recalled, still shocked by the answer. "It was something normal for them, they were used to it."

Parsa said his confinement in "mall jail" reminded him of the KGB. Yet the Mall of America's hostility to a Christian pastor sharing his testimony seemed even more familiar to the Iranian refugee.

"I've gone through this before — in Muslim countries I was arrested for passing out bibles," Parsa said. "I didn't expect that would happen in America. As a citizen in America, I have rights. They denied my basic rights."

<u>https://creepingsharia.wordpress.com/2019/02/10/mall-of-america-sharia/</u>

The name of Alexandra Natapoff's book (in the Bibliography) is exceedingly appropriate for what has gone wrong with our Department of Justice – ***Punishment Without Crime*** – and it costs all of us in one way or another.

Chapter 12

Plea Bargaining or Government Protected Blackmail?

Plea bargaining is defined as "The making of an agreement between a criminal defendant and the prosecutor that allows the defendant to plead guilty to a lesser charge, thereby avoiding the risk of a more severe sentence."[1]

Sounds good, doesn't it? It sounds so very fair too. But reading between the lines, that definition assumes that the defendant is guilty of a crime beyond a reasonable doubt. It means that there is enough evidence to reasonably convince a jury to make the decision of guilty.

All too frequently that is *not* the case.

Even in a situation where there wasn't a crime committed or when there is little or no evidence to prove that the defendant committed that crime, often the prosecutor will still attempt to get the defendant to plead guilty.

Again, the reason may be for the benefit of the prosecutor. It may be for the prosecutor who wants to achieve a personal, professional, and/or a political goal.

My resources led me to conclude that plea bargaining was frequently at the crux of someone "copping a plea" even though innocent. (The other instance in which someone will plead guilty although innocent is during a police interrogation.)

Several books and online articles described plea bargaining as a form of torture.[1] There are various reasons why innocent people plead guilty. But it almost always adds up to tremendous pressure, threats, and intimidation by a prosecutor. Even in my little case, when the prosecutor threatened to charge me with a crime for the second time, her "plea bargain" was a more severe punishment than the first time. Of course, if I refused to cop to her demands, I knew that she would officially charge me and back to court we would go. That meant the media would again do what they do.

Paul Craig Roberts and Lawrence M.
Stratton, *The Tyranny of Good Intentions*

Plea bargaining does not require any concern about truth.

But It Works on TV

Oh, I know. Who doesn't love it when a prosecutor lays into a bad guy with severe threats unless he or she confesses to the crime? On TV the prosecutor is portrayed as the hero while the defense attorney is depicted as something akin to a snake oil salesman (or woman) replete with greased back hair and ulterior motives.

Typically, the prosecutor is the defender of the innocent and the law. He/she always follows the law. The defendant is given his/her constitutional rights throughout the whole process. The prosecutor always acts in the best interest of the citizens. Any information that would clear the defendant of charges is immediately given to the defense attorney. The TV prosecutor would never lie, cheat, or charge someone with a crime for a political, personal, or professional reason but only for a legitimate crime and indeed observe the long-held legal principle of mens rea (criminal intent).

But, on TV, we already know that the bad guy is guilty. We

already know the truth. In the real world, prosecutors, often, don't know the truth, and/or they don't care about truth.

Plea bargaining is legitimate in some cases. It does save the taxpayers the expense of a trial. Plea bargaining is positive when used in a case where the predominance of evidence indicates that the person is guilty of a crime—and that, statutorily, a crime was committed. When the prosecution is convinced that they have enough evidence to convict beyond a reasonable doubt in a trial, offering a plea rather than an expensive trial is serving justice as well as saving taxpayer money.

In our current court system, plea bargaining, however, is often used to give the prosecutor what he or she wants regardless of the truth. Because plea bargaining has been so accepted, because both attorneys will agree to a plea bargain, and because a judge will also agree, justice; truth may or may not be served.

Looking at definitions and the Wisconsin State statutes, it certainly appears that when there is little or no evidence of a crime or when no crime was committed at all, plea bargaining is really blackmailing.

Blackmail:

Extortion or coercion by threats especially of public exposure or criminal prosecution; payment that is extorted.[2]

Blackmail involves a threat to do something that would cause a person to suffer embarrassment or financial loss, unless that person meets certain demands. The threat might include:

- to reveal private information about a person that is likely to cause them embarrassment (such as getting misleading and embarrassing information in the media where one is assumed guilty until proven innocent);

- to reveal sensitive information that is likely to cause

financial harm (pay this fine and give up your personal property or else);

- to accuse a person falsely of a crime (threats to issue a criminal charge for no legal reason); or to report a person's involvement in a crime.[3]

Wisconsin State Statute 943.30

Threats to injure or accuse of crime

Whoever, either verbally or by any written or printed communication, maliciously threatens to accuse or accuses another of any crime or offense, or threatens or commits any injury to the person, property, business, profession, calling or trade, or the profits and income of any business, profession, calling or trade of another, with intent thereby to extort money or any pecuniary advantage whatever, or with intent to compel the person so threatened to do any act against the person's will or omit to do any lawful act, is guilty of a Class H felony.

Wisconsin State Statute 943.31

Threats to communicate derogatory information

Whoever maliciously threatens, with intent to extort money or any pecuniary advantage whatever, or with intent to compel the person so threatened to do any act against the person's will, to disseminate or to communicate to anyone information, whether true or false, that would humiliate or injure the reputation of the threatened person or another is guilty of a Class I felony.

In my case and in many others, truth—even when known by the prosecutor—doesn't matter. Had I "copped to a plea" and lied to the court saying I was guilty when I wasn't, my lie would be accepted by the court. That lie would be wholly accepted by both attorneys and the judge. There may even be the knowledge that there is not enough evidence to convict, but that means nothing. And my Fifth Amendment right to not incriminate myself doesn't count.

*"No person…shall be compelled in any criminal case
to be a witness against himself, nor be deprived of life,
liberty, or property, without due process of law…"*

Fifth Amendment of the US Constitution

When plea bargaining is used as it was in my case and in other cases, how can it be labeled anything but blackmail? In my case, statutorily there was no crime, there was no criminal intent, no one was harmed.[4]

According to the Center for Prosecutor Integrity, a "plea bar-gained" innocent person is often wrongly convicted and may serve jail sentences for ten, twenty, or more years.[5] This person was blackmailed into admitting guilt and was finally proven innocent by DNA evidence, recanted witness statements (originally coerced by prosecutors), or exculpatory evidence found that the prosecutor hid from the defense attorney.

The entire justice system revolves around the prosecutor, a fallible human, who way too often is charging someone with a crime based on their own agenda regardless of the law, the Constitution, or the rule of law.

*"Prosecutors are the most powerful officials in the criminal justice
system. They decide whether criminal charges should be brought
and what those charges should be, and they exercise almost
boundless discretion in making those crucial decisions. Prosecutors*

alone decide whether to offer the defendant the option of pleading guilty to reduced charges. When one considers the fact that more than 95 percent of all criminal cases are resolved with guilty pleas, it is very clear that prosecutors control the criminal justice system through their charging and plea-bargaining powers."

Angela J. Davis, "The Power and Discretion
of the American Prosecutor"

If more of us don't wake up, we will have the legal system of a tyrannical government. I cannot help but wonder if we are already more than halfway there.

Blackmail is illegal. Yet, a prosecutor can essentially blackmail anyone for any reason and call it plea bargaining. The misuse of plea bargaining has become so ingrained into the justice system that no one seems to consider, for even one moment, that it is frequently not in the best interest of "we the people."

"The most significant criticism of plea bargaining is that plea bargaining can coerce innocent defendants into pleading guilty. The prosecutor's unlimited discretion to pick and choose which charges to bring against defendants and ability to create significant sentencing differentials between similar defendants can lead to the practice of overcharging and the use of threats to seek the harshest sentence to keep defendants from going to trial.

It sure is a sad state when we have a criminal justice system that purports to uphold the Constitutional liberties of its defendants, but surreptitiously forces most of them to waive away these rights…, prosecutors take on the role of judge and jury…The end result is a decision that has little to do with the primary objectives of the criminal justice system."

The Unnecessary Evil of Plea Bargaining… Tina Wan J.D.

Plea Bargaining Hides Truth from the Public

Had I accepted a plea bargain, no one would have known that, according to the written law, a crime was never committed. If I had been willing to lie, the prosecutor's dealings during the pre-charge interview would have stayed behind closed doors. This book would have never been written. I would have had a criminal record for no legal reason and, no doubt would have carried this undeserved label around for the rest of my life.

How many other cases have stayed "safely" behind the closed doors of the Department of Justice?

Plea bargaining hides the details that would allow the public to observe what our justice system has become instead of what it was meant to be. In fact, I was told that whatever happens between a prosecutor and the accused—which includes, of course, the details of a plea bargain—are sacrosanct.

WHOA! My response to that was: "Don't I have a constitutional right to free speech?" The First Amendment.

I was reluctantly told: "Yes."[6]

"Equally problematic is the fact that the charging and plea-bargaining decisions are made behind closed doors, and prosecutors are not required to justify or explain these decisions to anyone. If a prosecutor treats two similarly situated defendants differently—charging one but not the other or offering a better plea offer to one—it is almost impossible to challenge such differential treatment. The lack of transparency in the prosecution function also leads to misconduct, like the failure to turn over exculpatory evidence—a common occurrence made famous by the prosecutors in the Duke lacrosse and Senator Ted Stevens cases."

Angela J. Davis, "The Power and Discretion
of the American Prosecutor"

Before we go to the next chapter, I want to establish that I did not write this book for any kind of revenge. This issue is far bigger and broader than just me. There is a proverb: "When you go to bury your enemy, take two shovels." How true! And as a Christian, I know that vengeance doesn't belong to me.

Notes Chapter 12

1   "Plea bargaining," Legal Dictionary, https://legaldictionary.
net/plea-bargaining/
Plea bargaining as torture was covered in several of the books
and online article I read. If you do a search—plea bargain
and torture—you will get many articles.

2   "Blackmail," Merriam Webster, https://www.merriam-
webster.com/dictionary/blackmail

3   "Blackmail," Justia, https://www.justia.com/criminal/
offenses/white-collar-crimes/blackmail/

4   The prosecutor's "plea bargains" involved the confiscation
of my personal property (my firearm) and my money (a fine),
and admitting to a crime when, according to the written law,
a crime never occurred. I would forever have a record of
committing a crime and being a criminal unless I acquiesced
to her demands, in which my property, money, and my
reputation would be taken—extorted.
Her "plea bargain" for the second charge was my personal
property (my firearm), more of my money (a fine) than what
she wanted for the first charge, taking away my Second
Amendment rights for a specified period of time, and
admitting to a crime when I didn't commit one.
After the public condemnation of her prosecutorial overreach
by Wisconsin Carry and the subsequent complaints via email,
mail, and phone calls, she offered the "kinder, gentler" plea
bargain, which essentially was less of my money and less time
without my Second Amendment rights.
In my most humble opinion, that is a lot of power for a tax-
paid employee to have over a citizen of this country and this
state. It certainly seems to fit the definition of blackmail.

5   From the Center for Prosecutor Integrity:
Fact #1: Since 1989, there have been over 2,400
documented cases of persons who have been convicted and
later exonerated (1).

Fact #2: An estimated 43% of wrongful convictions arise from misconduct involving prosecutors, police, investigators, and other officials (1).

Fact #3: More than 90% of criminal cases are adjudicated during closed-door plea-bargain negotiations. These cases have little or no public accountability (2).

Fact #4: The following are the most common types of ethical violations committed by prosecutors (3):

- Failure to disclose exculpatory evidence (Brady violation)
- Use of inadmissible or false evidence/lack of candor to the court
- Plea bargain offense
- Inflammatory statements/witness harassment
- Mischaracterizing the evidence
- Vouching

Fact #5: Fewer than 2% of cases of prosecutor misconduct are subject to public sanctions. When sanctions are imposed, they are often slight (4).

Fact #6: Americans are concerned about the fairness of our criminal justice system (5).

Citations:

1. National Registry of Exonerations, UPDATE: 2012 The National Registry of Exonerations, April 3, 2013.

2. Sapien J. and Hernandez S. Who Polices Prosecutors Who Abuse Their Authority? Usually Nobody.

3. Center for Prosecutor Integrity. Registry of Prosecutorial Misconduct.

4. Center for Prosecutor Integrity. An Epidemic of Prosecutor Misconduct. Appendix B (2013).

5. Center for Prosecutor Integrity. Most Americans Doubt Fairness of Criminal Justice System, Reveals Center for Prosecutor Integrity. June 11, 2013.

6. Thank you, Eric O'Keefe, for demanding your First Amendment rights to speak out about what was done to the innocent targets of the John Doe case investigation. When you were told that you could not tell anyone what prosecutor

DA John Chisholm has inflicted on you and the rest of the targeted citizens, you spoke out and the rest followed. Your brave and proper move gave me the confidence to do the same.

There are prosecutors who want to do the right thing. They want to practice their professions in the best interest of the people and not of themselves
It is interesting to note that the Innocence Project's attorneys are, for the first time, representing a prosecutor. There is a law for prosecutors called the Brady Law which says that prosecutors may not hide exculpatory evidence from the defense attorney. That is any evidence obtained by the prosecutor that would prove the defendant's innocence. Prosecutors frequently do so anyway and are not charged for breaking this law i.e. committing a crime.

"Innocence Project attorneys will argue Wednesday, October 31, 2018 in Texas Supreme Court on behalf of a former Texas prosecutor who was wrongly fired when he refused to follow an illegal order to hide potentially exculpatory evidence from a defendant.

After he was fired for refusing to "follow orders," Hillman sued to get his job back, arguing that Texas law should protect prosecutors who refuse to break the law and hide evidence that aids the defense.

This is the first time in its twenty-seven-year history that the Innocence Project has appeared in court or filed a brief on behalf of a current or former prosecutor.

"Eric Hillman put his livelihood on the line to do the right thing. He should have been celebrated for his commitment to justice, not fired and forced out of his dream job as a prosecutor," *said Nina Morrison, senior staff attorney at the Innocence Project.*

Chapter 13

Is This Any Way to Treat a Lady?

Lady Justice

The following is a summary of several definitions for the symbolism of Lady Justice:

- The blindfold symbolizes that justice is blind. Justice is supposed to be objective. Justice is blind to who she is judging. Therefore, justice judges with reason and rationality.
- The scales of justice is the symbol that it is the "weight of the evidence" that decides a verdict. Fairness takes into account both sides and weighs the evidence with reason and rationality.
- The sword in most depictions of Lady Justice is held down. This was meant to mean that power is acquiescent to justice. Unless power is "wielded" judiciously it is arbitrary.[1]

Intuition and, ultimately, years of research, convinced me that I was not treated justly. I joined the many others who are speaking out either because of experiencing unjust treatment or having awareness of cases where injustice ruled. Once exposed to the pervasive amount of injustice carried out by prosecutors, it is difficult not to be appalled at the number of people who have suffered. Therefore, I had to try to get justice for an injustice.

Does the symbol for our justice system mean something or is it just a symbol for what was but is no more?

I had to find out for myself if it was true that no one would hold prosecutors accountable; no one would levy consequences for injustice.

Who Ya Gonna Call?

While the Ghostbusters[2] dealt with something that wasn't real as if it were real, it appears that the Wisconsin Supreme Court's Office of Lawyer Regulation deals with something real as if it isn't real—at least, in my case. The Office of Lawyer Regulation is who you call when an attorney commits an ethics violation. This office, which is attached to the Wisconsin Supreme Court, is charged to investigate any ethical violations by lawyers.

They would not even investigate in my case.

Yes, they sent someone to ask the prosecutor about the two "no probable cause" criminal charges. That investigator deemed those two charges appropriate. The exact words of the investigator in her letter to me: "the prosecutor's charging decisions appear to have been the product of proper discretion and relevant facts." She didn't see any ethics violations.

Let's review the relevant facts:

- Two judges dismissed two charges as having no probable cause
- There is a Wisconsin State statute, i.e., a law written by the Legislative Branch of our government, that exactly describes what I unintendedly did as not being a crime.

Consequently, and logically:

- the prosecutor knew there was no probable cause. That is a violation of SCR 20:3.8(a): A prosecutor in a criminal case or a proceeding that could result in deprivation of liberty shall not prosecute a charge that the prosecutor knows is not supported by probable cause.
- or she didn't know, which could mean that she doesn't know the law and may not be qualified for the job.
- and/or she may have been attempting to make law therefore violating the separation of powers.
- the only facts the prosecutor expressed was that "the media got this," sending a message to the community, and that it troubled her. Those are not "...the product of proper discretion and relevant facts" for issuing a criminal charge
- my constitutional rights were violated.

I did refer to the Office of Lawyer Regulation what certainly seems like a legitimate case of an ethics violation by a prosecutor. "No probable cause" charges were not only issued once but twice.

> *"Indeed, when a prosecutor violates ethical precepts, judges and appellate seemingly bend over backward to excuse the conduct. Even in the most reprehensible cases, judges typically do not refer the case for disciplinary action, and ethics boards fail to apply sanctions. Courts rely upon fault-absolving notions like 'harmless error,' a doctrine that has been termed the 'lie that the criminal justice system tells itself.'"*

> Jim Dwyer et al., *Actual Innocence: When Justice Goes Wrong and How to Make it Right*

I wrote to the director of the Office of Lawyer Regulation and asked him to please reconsider. I appealed to have my ethics complaint investigated fully.

I was informed that there was probable cause for the prosecutor to issue two criminal charges because "bond was set." If setting bond—actually it was bail—was probable cause for a criminal charge, why is a judge even necessary? All you need is the court commissioner who rarely to never dismisses a case.

When a case is passed on to a judge by the court commissioner, bail is always set. That does not establish probable cause. You probably remember, the court commissioner used "somebody could have" as probable cause in the first criminal charge. For the second criminal charge, he didn't have to decide at all because both attorneys asked for a judge. Bail was set again, as is the procedure.

My next request to that office was to give me a legal reason as to why they would not investigate. I was mailed a case that supposedly established a precedent for the fact that bond being set established probable cause.

I may not be an attorney or have any formal training in the law; however, I can read, I can reason, and I can tell the difference between an apple and a turnip.

The case that was sent was about as far afield from any kind of precedent in my case as the cases the prosecutors used to establish mens rea. Sean Hannity sure did ask the right question; What do you do when the people who are supposed to hold others accountable refuse to do so?

Legal Options a Lawsuit?

Four elements must be present in a case to file a **malicious prosecution** charge.

1. The defendant (DA and ADA) commenced a criminal proceeding. (ADA did with DA approval -twice, two separate charges for the same thing)

2. The proceeding ended in the victim's favor (It did – twice)
3. There was no Probable Cause (there wasn't – twice)
4. The proceeding was brought with malice toward the victim. Or there was an improper purpose. Improper purpose can be inferred from an improbable cause. (appears to be true in my case) [3,4]

Did I have a case to file a malicious prosecution charge? Probably. But if I were to pursue a case, I would lose. No matter how strong and factual the evidence is, after spending thousands of dollars, I would fail. What are the chances of even finding an attorney who would represent me against a government prosecutor? Close to zero.

There is also a federal law called the **Color of Law**:[5]

TITLE 18, U.S.C., SECTION 242

Whoever, under color of any law, statute, ordinance, regulation, or custom willfully subjects any person in any State, Territory, Commonwealth, Possession, or District to the deprivation of any rights, privileges, or immunities secured or protected by the Constitution or laws of the United States, ... shall be fined under this title or imprisoned not more than one year, or both·

There is also **Wisconsin Code 946.12** that could be applicable and could be applied to ignoring the law that exactly covered the action as well as the possible attempt to make law.

Wisconsin State Statute 946.12

Misconduct in public office

(2) In the officer's or employee's capacity as such officer or employee, does an act which the officer or employee knows is in

excess of the officer's or employee's lawful authority or which the officer or employee knows the officer or employee is forbidden by law to do in the officer's or employee's official capacity;

(3) Whether by act of commission or omission, in the officer's or employee's capacity as such officer or employee exercises a discretionary power in a manner inconsistent with the duties of the officer's or employee's office or employment or the rights of others and with intent to obtain a dishonest advantage for the officer or employee or another.

Sounds possible, right? I'd lose.

I could try **abuse of power,** defined as "improper use of authority by someone who has that authority because he or she holds a public office."[6]

When a prosecutor uses "the media got this" as well as the written statement that it "troubled her" as probable cause for two criminal charges, that certainly seems like an abuse of power. Neither you nor I could institute a criminal charge against someone because of the media or because something troubled us. Only a prosecutor, because of a job with virtually absolute legal immunity, could do that.

Were My Civil Rights Violated?

The Fourteenth Amendment addresses many aspects of citizenship and the rights of citizens. The most commonly used, and frequently litigated phrase, in the amendment is "equal protection of the laws." Obviously, I did not get equal protection of the laws.

First, the written law was ignored.

Second, there was at least one person who was never criminally charged for forgetting his firearm in a public place. That person, in the jurisdiction of the Waukesha County Department of Justice, was not charged with a crime by the same DA who allowed two criminal charges to be made against me.

(And, by the way, there were other cases in other Wisconsin counties that had been reported in the media of people forgetting their guns in a public place yet never being charged with a crime.)

> *"A federal charge of depriving the defendants of their civil rights would get to the same issues by a different route. According to federal statute, it is a crime for any person acting "under color of law" to willfully deprive a person of a constitutional right. Acting "under color of law" essentially means using the power of the government, and* ***it includes the actions of state prosecutors in criminal cases. The constitutional right at issue would be the defendants' well-established due process… Deliberately depriving a defendant of his constitutional rights is a crime if you believe him to be guilty"***. (Findlaw.com)

During the years of investigating the many different legal possibilities in my attempt to get justice while continuing research on prosecutor misconduct and abuse, I soon realized that I could take all the money we have and all the rest of the years of my life to attempt to get justice via a lawsuit and would still net zero.

Our Elected (Alleged) Public Servants?

In the Bill of Rights First Amendment, we have the right to petition our government for redress of grievances. A redress of grievance means resolving a problem—essentially, the right to petition the government to solve a problem.

In petitioning the government for redress of a grievance, it seemed logical that I should start with the government body and the elected official closest to my problem of seeking justice for an injustice.

I started with the DA. I began with letters and never got a response. Then, I approached him in person. It was the grand opening of the new Wisconsin Firearms Training Center in Brookfield, WI on March 5, 2016. The DA was there and spoke to the group attending.

After he spoke, I approached him, introduced myself, and handed him the book *The Tyranny of Good Intentions* along with copies of some of the research I had done on prosecutor misconduct.

As I began to ask him a question, he maneuvered around me and walked away. The DA who was, at that time, the attorney general of Wisconsin, never said one word to me. I called after him: "We have a problem here, Mr. _____." He just kept walking, and I did not see him again.

Just walk away DA?

I don't blame him. We both knew that he had no way of defending even one of those criminal charges, let alone two.

This is a man with a law degree, who passed the Bar, who had been a district attorney and then Wisconsin's attorney general. It seems unbelievable that he didn't know that either of the criminal charges that he allowed did not have a probable cause—a legal reason for ever being issued. When he was the DA in Waukesha County, he had at least one other person who did the same thing that I did, and he did not issue a criminal charge. He must have known the same law this "non-attorney granny" found without any problem when searching the Wisconsin State statutes.

In writing and verbally, I have heard this man state that as district attorney and as attorney general, he was and is a strict Constitutionalist.[7] He has also written and said that he follows the rule of law.

Call Your Legislator?

I couldn't get the official office (the Office of Lawyer Regulation), charged to investigate reported lawyer ethics violations, to even fully investigate. I'd go broke attempting to file a lawsuit. In 2014 the DA, the person who had the power to stop a no probable cause criminal charge, refused to talk with me.

So, I decided to research how to approach the lawmakers—i.e., our Legislative Branch of government—and attempt to change the law of granting prosecutors absolute immunity to qualified immunity.

> *"Court's prosecutorial misconduct jurisprudence leads inevitably to the conclusion that a broad reexamination is warranted. Such a reexamination would weigh heavily in favor of permitting prosecutors to be held liable for acts of misconduct committed, provided the law clearly established that the acts constituted misconduct. In other words,* **prosecutors should have qualified, not absolute, immunity.** *"*
>
> Malia N. Brink, *A Pendulum Swung Too Far*

Although I had been striking out with our public servants so far, I called my legislator. My legislator told me that he would have to connect me with a drafting attorney. But he stated that he didn't have time for that now. He would do that after the next session.

That became his standard answer to me for approximately one year. That is when he did return my phone calls, which was rare.

I wrote to Governor Walker and asked him what to do when your representative won't represent you. Shortly after, I got a call from one of legislator's staff members who was condescending, patronizing, and just plain rude. At first, the staff member curtly asked me to email her with my request in one sentence. Although that was certainly difficult to do, I did it. I received no response from her. I called her. She couldn't talk but would call me back. She didn't.

I called her after waiting more than a respectful amount of time. She told me to write my senator because getting the senate involved too would be good. I did that. In my first letter, I spelled my senator's name incorrectly. I immediately wrote another letter apologizing for the incorrect spelling.

I waited and waited for the staff member to call. She didn't so I called her. The staff member upbraided me for spelling the senator's name wrong. She also scolded me for mentioning that my legislator suggested that I contact my senator. Apparently, I wasn't supposed to do that. Her message to me was clear – I had been a very bad private citizen.

Another letter went to Governor Walker.

Finally, my legislator called me asking me what was it that I wanted him to do. I asked if I could use his name to contact the legislator who was now on the committee he had been on. I did contact that person, who saw no reason to talk with me. I asked one more time, got the same answer, and gave up on him.

Did Any Elected Government Officials Respond?

Governor Scott Walker did.

Senator David Craig did.

Senator Craig isn't even my senator. But he had a staff member talk to me and ask what it was regarding. Since he is interested in constitutional rights, he agreed to see me. I was so accustomed to not even getting an acknowledgment to a letter or a phone call, let alone actually having someone agree to see me, that I was stunned.

Thanks Governor Walker. Thanks Senator Craig. You were both a spark of hope in a dismal search for help from my elected alleged public servants. You acted as actual public servants.

Several more contacts with legislators who were on the appropriate committees to help resulted in no responses.

By this time, after approximately three years of various attempts to get justice, I stopped trying—for a while. I could have contacted Senator Craig again, but I was confused about the best way to seek legislative assistance. I wasn't sure if there was a better route to go.

Yes, I was fighting back, but it was like a bee attempting to sting a marble statue.

Hi, I'm from Your Government and I'm Here to Help

At some point, all government bureaucracies and all large businesses become self-protective and self-serving. They forget who they are charged to serve. I believe it is more so with the government than with a private business. If a private business angers too many people, it will go out of business. The government has all the money it needs to do whatever it wants—they have us. They have our money.

I have been attentive to happenings in our government. I have been politically active in various ways. That was true for me even before being criminally charged for not committing a crime.

Prosecutor misconduct, the use and abuse of innocent people by government employees, had become personal. I personally experienced what so many others before have. I could not just forget it. Yes, it was technically over for me. But it wasn't over for the next person, and the next person and…

Now What?

As previously stated, Pastor Stuart Briscoe has said that in a sermon, or when you are reading and studying the Bible, three questions need addressing:

- What? (…Is it about?)
- So What? (How does it pertain to you?)
- Now What? (…Are you going to do about it?)

For me the *What* was a personal experience. The *So What* was the collateral damage done to me by one of our branches of our government that certainly appears to be exercising tyrannical and arbitrary power. For others, the *So What* is that this has happened to many people and could happen to anyone—for almost anything—at any time.

The *Now What* took various ways to obtain justice. All of which failed.

There is the old saying: "If what you are doing isn't working, do something else." By late 2017, I began to realize that I needed a way to tell my story fully. I also knew it was imperative that more people realized that anyone could be next. More people needed to know that they could be a target of a prosecutor with an agenda other than the law.

A book by an unknown, previously unpublished author may not do much to change the reality of what our justice system has become. I am another voice, however, in attempting to wake up the public to the danger of losing more and more of our liberty and freedom.

The Department of Justice has all but forgotten about justice. In their efforts to use power to achieve personal, professional, political goals, too many prosecutors and judges are more interested in getting what they want than protecting the safety and freedom of the citizens of America.

What was once the symbol for a country that represented freedom, liberty, and justice for all no longer seems to fit.

"Apparently, it's (the blindfold's) original significance was that the judicial system was tolerating abuse or ignorance of aspects of the law" [8]

It seems that the original significance is appropriate once again.

Our symbol of a fair and just Judicial Branch of government is tarnished with disrespect for the best interest of the citizens of America.

This just isn't any way to treat a lady; this isn't the way our justice system was originally meant to treat anyone.

So…what now?

Notes Chapter 13

1   A worthwhile study is to understand how our legal system
    went from being a shield to protect the citizen to a sword
    that all too frequently harms the citizen. The law is currently
    being used too often as a sword for social control.
    The two legal minds that disagreed with one another were
    Blackstone (the shield) and Bentham (the sword). The book,
    Tyranny of Good Intentions, in my bibliography provides an
    excellent discussion of each.
2   Ghostbusters movie Director: Ivan Reitman Writers: Dan
    Aykroyd, Harold Ramis.
3   "Malicious prosecution," The Free Dictionary, https://legal –
    dictionary- the free-   dictionary.com/Elements+of+Proof
4   "Malicious prosecution," Law Library – American Law
    & Legal Information, https://law.jrank.org/pages/8403/
    Malicious-Prosecution-Elements-Proof.html
5   "Deprivation of Rights Under Color of Law," The United
    States Department of Justice, https://www.justice.gov/crt/
    deprivation-rights-under-color-law
6   "Abuse of power," The Free Dictionary, https://legal-
    dictionary.thefreedictionary.com/Abuse+of+Power
7   On July 1, 2014 on the Vicki McKenna show DA Brad
    Schmiel said this: " A DA cannot be expected to police
    themselves, the Constitution is all important."
8   https://heatherandlittle.com/blog/restoration/
    the-meaning-behind-the-lady-of-justice-statue/

*In Wisconsin, both the Office of Lawyer Regulation (OLR) and
Wisconsin Judicial Commission (WJC) are bad jokes upon the public,
or better stated by my friend as feckless. They are whitewashing agencies
established to protect their peers - the accused.*

*All complaints are kept confidential unless acted upon. These agencies are
exempt from Open Record Laws and lack any degree of accountability.*

Time to make these policing agencies accountable to the public. State

*Senator David Craig could be point man on this project to draft
legislation to remove these agencies from the Wisconsin Supreme Court
and hold the agencies accountable to the public.*
(Political Activist Harry Wait)http://racinecountycorruption.
blogspot.com/)

Chapter 14

Now What?

"First, Do No Harm"

American Bar Association

First, do no harm

Volume 29 Number 3

Allan Head

" First, do no harm"

I wasn't sure I had heard it right, but sure enough, that was what he (Superior Court Judge Don Stephens) said, to 107 newly licensed lawyers as he administered the oath.

"First, do no harm"… to our profession, to the client we represent, and to the community in which we live.

"If you compromise these principles, you will do great harm to yourself, your profession, ultimately to your client, and certainly to your community."

We have a Department of Justice, at all levels, harming innocent people, assassinating their character, making them spend copious amounts of money to defend bogus criminal charges, ruining lives, and committing acts that are immoral, unethical, cruel, callous, and merciless.

I realize that these are especially strong words. Simply looking at the titles of many of the books in my bibliography will underline why these words are backed by factual cases and experiences. *A lot* of them.

The people like Jim in Sidney Powell's book, the targets, victims of DA John Chisholm's ordered early-morning raids on private homes, the people who have been incarcerated for decades because a prosecutor hid evidence that would have cleared him or her... All of these people and many more were innocent of committing any crimes.

That is why the Center for Prosecutor Integrity can call prosecutor misconduct an epidemic. Prosecutorial abuse is rampant. It's not just a few cases here and there.

Who Cares?

Unfortunately, it seems to be only those who have directly experienced the collateral damage done to them by the abuse of power by prosecutors or those who have observed it who care.

More of us need to wake up and realize that anyone could be next.

Any one of us could be the next person to have our lives harshly altered by the collateral damage caused by a prosecutor who is free to exercise absolute, arbitrary power with no accountability.

It's About Time... To Change a
System That Has Gone Wrong

Please consider joining me in informing more people of the dangerous functioning of our current justice system. Unless or until there is awareness and insistence for change from more and more of us, the epidemic of prosecutor misconduct will only increase.

My plan is to give away as many books as I can to elected government officials; people in written, online, and television news; pertinent organizations; and people in the local and national DOJ—and anyone else who can be of help in instituting change in a criminal justice system, a branch of our government that has strayed far afield from its original intent.

If you want to help increase awareness of the relatively unknown danger to our liberty and freedoms, pass your book on to someone else. Or, if you want to and if you can, purchase a book to give to someone else, a friend, your senator or representative, or…

With every two or three books purchased, I can buy another book to give away. That is a huge step to increasing awareness and encouraging action in fighting the growing tyranny of our justice system via prosecutors. (Books available on Amazon and other online booksellers.)

I would have never bought and read the books that I did if I had not personally experienced what I did at the hands of a prosecutor.

By purchasing another book, it not only helps me purchase more to give away, but it also adds another person who will be aware that prosecutors do use innocent people for their own reasons rather than for a legal one. That may spur more people to take action for change.

If you are like me, your inbox is filled with requests for donations from many worthy causes. I would love to donate to all of them. But I can't. Who can? I have chosen several to which I donate via monthly contributions online.

So, purchasing a book is the only monetary help for which I will ask.

You can join my email list at Susan@GoToJustGrandma.com. You will get emails a few times a month.

You will be informed of:

- recent initiatives on holding prosecutors accountable for misconduct
- new and pertinent information relating to the criminal justice system

- any new cases of innocent people being criminally charged by
  a prosecutor with an agenda other than the law
- sometimes, a request to send an email or make a phone call

I chose the name Just Grandma for my email and my website—*just* as in simply and *just* as in justice.

You may also visit my website www.GoToJustGrandma.com.

Please email me about you personally, someone you know, or someone you read or heard about where you suspect that there might be prosecutor If I can help in any way—even if it means sending them a free book—I will.

What Needs to Happen?

These necessary changes in order to deal with the epidemic of prosecutor misconduct and damage to individual people, taxpayers, and the system itself were consistently mentioned in my research:

- Give prosecutors qualified immunity, not absolute immunity
- Mandate and strengthen the requirement of mens rea (intent)
- Require consequences for the violation of constitutional rights
- Establish a review board/commission on prosecutor misconduct to which wronged citizens can appeal
- Require, at least, yearly training on ethical and constitutional conduct for prosecutors
- Stop rewarding prosecutors who commit misconduct, violate the rule of law, violate constitutional rights, violate ethical rules, attempt to make law, and/or hide exculpatory evidence
- Start rewarding prosecutors who issue honest, legal, legitimate charges and obtain convictions by observing all the protections put in place for the safety and best interest of the citizens

This will not be easy or immediate! Several states have begun calling for legislation to deal with the tyrannical power of prosecutors. New York is the first state that I know of to advocate for a prosecutorial commission to deal with prosecutor misconduct and recommend discipline.[1]

In Wisconsin, the only resource to report to and who can levy consequences for an ethical violation by a prosecutor is the Office of Lawyer Regulation. As written, in my case, they would not even investigate. All indications are that prosecutors are not going to regulate themselves. And, it appears that they will fight any attempt to be held accountable.

Change Only Happens When Enough People Demand It

I think it is safe to say that many of us are alarmed at how many actual criminals are given free passes. Sadly, some will go back into society and harm more people. But I would have never known that innocent people can be harmed by the same system that, far too often, gives soft treatment to actual criminals and even allow them to go free.

Please join me in educating more people to the fact that any of us, although totally innocent of committing a crime, can be used and abused by the most powerful people in the criminal justice system for their own purposes: the prosecutor.

*"There may be times when we are powerless to prevent injustice,
but there must never be a time when we fail to protest."*

Elie Wiesel

Notes Chapter 14

1   The most active group that I know of is It Could Happen to You (founder Bill Bastuk) in New York (www. itcouldhappen2you.org). Their stated solutions to the problem of prosecutor misconduct is legislation and public awareness.

From the It Could Happen to You website:

"OUR TENETS AND OUR STRATEGY"

You could be falsely accused.

You are innocent until proven guilty.

You are legally entitled to all evidence in the prosecutor's possession prior to presentation.

You, the accused, should have your name protected from the public until either convicted or acquitted.

Falsely accusing you threatens the community at large allowing the true felon to stay on the streets and commit other crimes.

I am grateful to Mr. Bastuk for fighting back as well as providing me with an excellent model and example.

From the It Could Happen to You website:

"OUR TENETS AND OUR STRATEGY

You could be falsely accused.

You are innocent until proven guilty.

You are legally entitled to all evidence in the prosecutor's possession prior to presentation.

You, the accused, should have your name protected from the public until either convicted or acquitted.

Falsely accusing you threatens the community at large allowing the true felon to stay on the streets and commit other crimes.

I am grateful to Mr. Bastuk for fighting back as well as providing me with an excellent model and example.

Naming the Unnamed

I struggled as to whether I should include the actual names of the people involved in my experience with the Waukesha, Wisconsin Department of Justice, Criminal Justice System. I decided that I would.

- **First**, it would be relativity simple to find out who the DA was in 2014.
- **Second**, the innocent people who are used by a prosecutor for that prosecutor's own purpose are publicly exposed via the media. That exposure punishes an innocent person in so many ways. Of course, they are, more than likely assumed to be guilty by the reading and viewing audience.
- **Third**, while innocent people are publicly exposed, the prosecutor who committed the misconduct not only is not held accountable but is protected from any public exposure. In other words, the "guilty party" remains anonymous.

The Prosecutor: Lesli S. Boese,
ADA (Assistant District Attorney) promoted
to DDA (Deputy District Attorney)

The DA: Brad Schimel

The Junior Prosecutor: Melissa J. Zilavy, ADA

The Court Commissioner: Thomas J. Pieper

The DA of Ozaukee County: Adam Gerol

The Director of the Office of Lawyer
Regulation: Keith Sellen

My Legislator: Joel Kleefisch

When our 23-year-old granddaughter (Mom of one of our 2 great grandchildren) was about 4 years old and planning to do something that she knew I would not approve, she would say: *"Grandma, close your eyes and close your back eyes too."*

It has been since the beginning that we humans want to hide certain things that we do. We want to do them behind closed doors and closed eyes (think Adam and Eve).

How many times have politicians proclaimed transparency in government?

How many times have we been assured of open records? Unless…

It certainly appears that government hiding out is an "age old" problem, as Paul said to the officers:

> *"They beat us publicly without a trial, even though we are Roman citizens, and threw us into prison. And now do they want to get rid of us quietly? No! Let them come themselves and escort us out."*

> Acts 16:37

"Our system of checks and balances depends on a vigorous judiciary and legislature serving as a brake on excessive prosecutorial zeal. It also depends on an alert private citizenry willing to exercise its constitutional right, indeed obligation, to petition the government for a redress of grievances."

Harvey A. Silverglate, *Three Felonies a Day*

Thanks To:

To my supportive family and friends

To my Christian sisters (Especially the 3 C's (Cheryl, Cindy, & Carol).

To the GWG—thank you for your support, your encouragement, our times together training, and going to lunch after.

To the "guys" at Fletcher Arms Range—you were understanding and instructive.

To the Heavenly Humble Helpful, many of whom didn't know me before this. And to those who considered themselves qualified to throw the first stone; the holier than thou (both helped frame this book).

To Harry and his blog Racine County Corruption (http:// racinecountycorruption.blogspot.com), Tom, and Barb, who expanded on what I had learned and who faithfully supported me in writing this book.

To my attorney—Tom Grieve—a perfect choice.

To Governor Scott Walker.

To Senator David Craig.

To Nik Clark and Wisconsin Carry.

To Eric O'Keefe and the other targets of the John Doe case for standing up and fighting back.

To Matt Kittle, formerly of Wisconsin Watchdog now with The MacIver Institute. You simplify complicated issues when you write, and I needed that!

To my husband, Jerry, who handled all food needs and did the dishes!

*To my editor, Kristen Hamilton—www.
kristencorrects.com. – I needed you*

*To those who went before and had the courage to speak out. You
gave me the confidence and courage to do the same.*

*To the man who called police on that "fateful" day. I know you felt bad
about doing so since you know us. But you gave me the opportunity to
experience Romans 8:28 and I am thankful. And to paraphrase Joseph
in Genesis 50:20: What was the unethical, immoral, unjust act of
people, "God intended it for good to accomplish what is now being done."*

*And always, eternal gratitude to my Lord and Savior who promised
He would never leave me of forsake me…and He never has.*

Bibliography

ABA Publishing. (2013). *Model Rules of Professional Conduct*. (2013 edition). USA: ABA Publishing.

Bach, A. (2009). *Ordinary Injustice: How America Holds Court*. (1st paperback edition). USA: Holt and Company.

Barton, D. (2003). *The Role of Pastors & Christians in Civil Government*. (1st edition, 5th printing, 2010). USA: WallBuilders.

Barton, D. (2013). *Original Intent: The Courts, the Constitution, and Religion*. (5th edition). USA: WallBuilders.

Beckman W. (2015). *Our Christian Founding Fathers: "…this is a Christian Nation."* (1st edition). USA: West Bow Press.

Bergman, J.D. Paul and Berman, J.D. Sara. (2015). *The Criminal Law Handbook: Know your Rights, Survive the System*. (14th edition). USA: Bang Printing.

Butler, P. (2009). *Let's Get Free: A Hip-Hop Theory of Justice*. (1st edition). USA: The New Press.

Chumley, C.K. (2014). *Police State U.S.A.: How Orwell's Nightmare is Becoming Our Reality*. (1st edition). USA: WND Books.

Daugherty, M.J. (2013). *The Devil Inside the Beltway: The Shocking Expose of the US Government's Surveillance and Overreach into Cybersecurity, Medicine and Small Business*. (1st edition). USA: Broadland Press.

Davis, A.J. (2007). *Arbitrary Justice: The Power of the American Prosecutor*. (1st paperback edition). USA: Oxford University Press.

Gershman, B.L. (2017). *Prosecution Stories: District Attorney El Dorado County*. (1st edition). USA: Twelve Tables Press.

Groseclose, T. (2011). *Left Turn: How Liberal Media Bias Distorts the American Mind*. (1st edition). USA: St. Martin's Press.

Hannity, S. (2004). *Deliver Us from Evil: Defeating Terrorism, Despotism, and Liberalism*. (1st edition). USA: Harper Collins Publications.

Healy, G. (2004). *Go Directly to Jail: The Criminalization of Almost Everything*. (1st edition). USA: Cato Institute.

Hillsdale College Politics Faculty. (2015). *The U.S. Constitution: A Reader.* (7th edition). USA: Hillsdale College Press.

Jackson, K. (2010). *The Cornered Cat: A Woman's Guide to Concealed Carry.* (1st edition). USA: White Feather Press.

Loesch, D. (2014). *Hands Off My Gun: Defeating the Plot to Disarm America.* (1st trade edition). USA: Center Street.

Lynch, T. (2009). *In the Name of Justice: Leading Experts Reexamine the Classic Article "The Aims of the Criminal Law."* (1st edition). USA: Cato Institute.

Napolitano, Judge A.P. (2004). *Constitutional Chaos: What Happens when the Government Breaks its own Laws.* (1st edition). USA: Nelson Current.

Napolitano, Judge A.P. (2011). *It is Dangerous to be Right When the Government is Wrong: The Case for Personal Freedom.* (1st edition). USA: Thomas Nelson.

Natapoff, Alexandra (2008). *Punishment Without Crime: How Our Massive Misdemeanor System Traps the Innocent and Makes America more Unequal.* Basic Books

Paine, T. (2001). *Common Sense and Related Writings: Thomas Paine.* (1st edition). USA: Bedford/St. Martin's.

Pollock, J.M. (2010). *Ethical Dilemmas and Decision in Criminal Justice.* (6th edition). Canada: Wadsworth, Cengage Learning.

Powell, S. (2014). *Licensed To Lie: Exposing Corruption in the Department of Justice.* (1st edition). USA: Brown Books Publishing Group.

Radelet, M.L. and Bedau, H.A. and Putnam, C.E. (1992). *In Spite of Innocence: The Ordeal of 400 Americans Wrongly Convicted of Crimes Punishable by Death.* (1st edition). USA: Northeastern University Press.

Roberts, P.C. and Stratton, L.M. (2008). *The Tyranny of Good Intentions: How Prosecutors and Law Enforcement are Trampling the Constitution in the Name of Justice.* (1st paperback edition). USA: Crown Publishing Group.

Rosenzweig, P. and Walsh, B.W. (2010). *One Nation Under Arrest: How Crazy Laws, Rogue Prosecutors, and Activist Judges Threaten your Liberty.* (1st edition). USA: The Heritage Foundation.

Schuelke, D. (2011). *Attorneys above the Law.* (1st edition). USA: Catchum Lion Enterprises, LLC.

Sekulow, J. (2015). *Undemocratic: How Unelected, Unaccountable*

Bureaucrats are Stealing your Liberty and Freedom. (1st edition).
USA: Howard Books.
Silvergate, H.A. (2009). *Three Felonies a Day: How the Fed's Target the
Innocent.* (1st edition). USA: Encounter Books.
Zinn, M. (1999). *Mad-Dog Prosecutors and other Hazards of American
Business: "Every American who Cares about Justice Should Read this
Book."* Alan M. Dershowitz. (5th edition). USA: Station Hill.

Printed in the USA
CPSIA information can be obtained
at www.ICGtesting.com
CBHW071800130724
PP15363900001B/2/J